i

beYOUtiful

MARTHA COTHRON

BeYOUtiful
Copyright © 2018 Martha Cothron

ISBN-13: 978-1983581588 (CreateSpace-Assigned)
ISBN-10: 1983581585

Cover Model/Photographer:
Martha Boss

Photographer:
Melissa McAnuff
Martha Cothron

Cover Designer:
Cover Crush Designs

Formatted by:
Brenda Wright, Formatting Done Wright

beYOUtiful

MARTHA COTHRON

Dedication

To my Sonda.
When the darkness came for me you kept me alive with your unconditional love.
Your voice lives through the pages of this book. It's all for you.
Tu me manques ma souer.

Foreword

Bonjour

You're reading this because I wrote it for you. I wrote it about you. It's packed with words of love and life lessons. Most people know me as "The Diva," but that's not who've I've always been. I walked through life not knowing who I was or who I wanted to be. I'm the chick who was always searching for my place in this crazy world full of banana peppers. I grew up the book-loving nerd with brown skin, abandonment issues, curly hair and a loud voice that commanded attention whenever I walked in a classroom. My aspiration in life has always been to be happy.

The journey of self love is never easy. Loving yourself fully means embracing your flaws and basking in your insecurities to a point where sometimes you just might want to scream and give up. When you're done reading this I want you to write yourself a letter and start it out, "Dear _____ (insert your name)." Fill it with truth and love for who God has made you. Hold on to it and open it 30 days from now. Be prepared to ask yourself these questions: How do you see yourself? What change did you make to help you focus on you?

I invited some of the greatest women I know to fill us with their knowledge and power on being beautiful. It's full of little stories of strength, poems of truth, quotes of happiness and most of all, LOVE. Love for all my sisters young and seasoned. You will also find some of the most beautiful pictures taken by photographer Melissa McAnuff.

This book is a nugget of me wanting every soul in the world to know they are diamonds. You have the right to shine. It's about me loving myself, loving you, loving everyone, exactly how they need to be loved. We are all beautiful it just takes the love of others around us to bring it to light. Know that I wish you all the best. Life is full of success and happiness. After all the darkness and sadness we experience throughout our lives, it's important to know happiness still comes.

Surround yourself with positive things and people. Be kind to yourself. Love your body. Embrace who God made you be. #beYOUtiful.

xoxo

Martha

Table of Contents

Part I

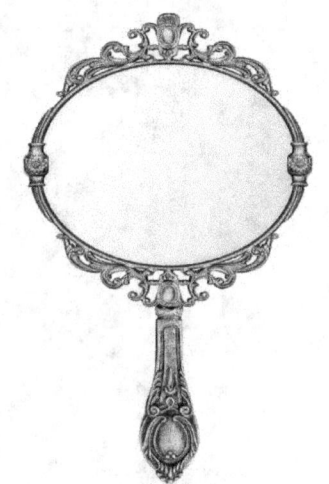

Le coup de foundre

(Love at first sight)

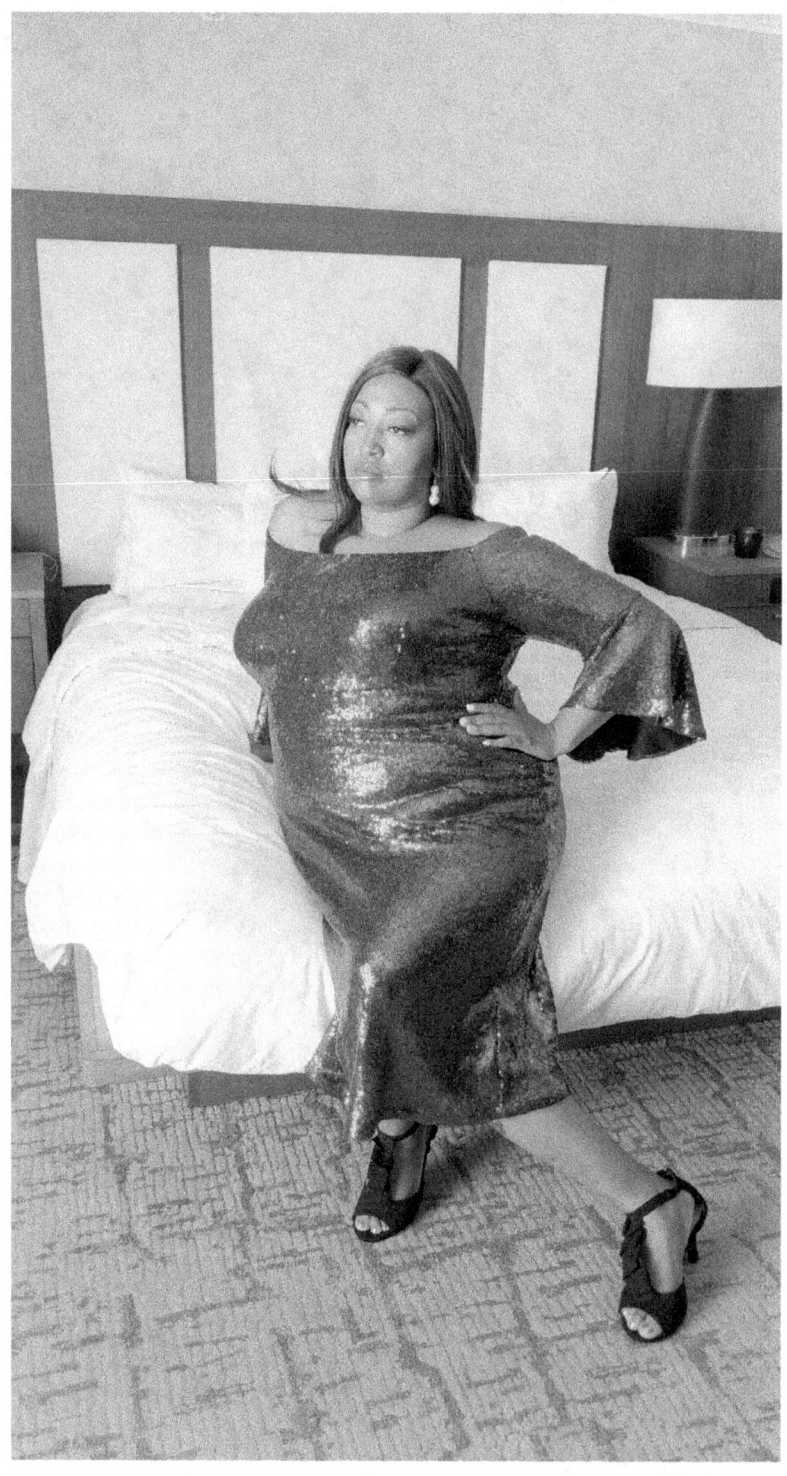

"Our deepest fear is not that we are inadequate. Our deepest fear is that we are powerful beyond measure. It is our Light, not our Darkness that most frightens us. We ask ourselves, who am I to be brilliant, gorgeous, talented, fabulous? Actually, who are you NOT to be? You are a child of God. Your playing small does not serve the world. There is nothing enlightening about shrinking so that other people won't feel unsure around you. We were born to make manifest the glory of God that is within us. It is not just in some of us; it is in everyone. As we let our own Light shine, we unconsciously give other people permission to do the same. As we are liberated from our own fear, our presence automatically liberates others."

Marianne Williamson

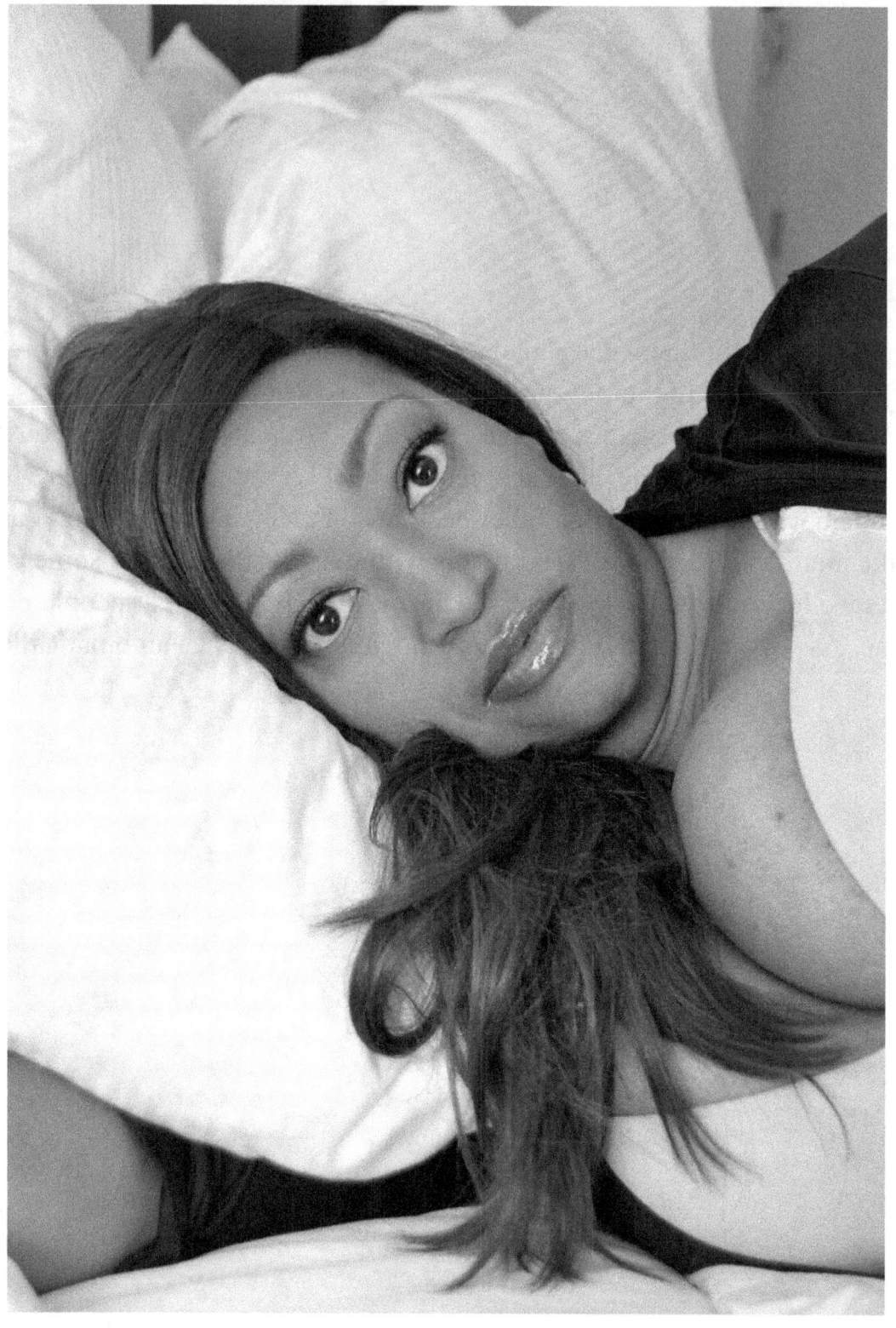

My First Time

The first time a I got my heart broken I thought I was going to die. The narcissist broke my love and trust into a million tiny shards of porcelain glass. He cheated on me. I found out from a friend who found out from a friend who found out from the girl he was cheating on me with on AOL Instant Messenger. What she described to me was all of him. The EX. The man who broke me and left me to die.

Why? Why did he leave me to die rotting in my own self doubt that he help create? Because he didn't care. He had me any which way he wanted me and it wasn't enough for him. He broke me and watched me crumble at his Air Jordans like the weeping willow that he turned me into.

But you know what? I let him. I let him cut to the quick. I let him think that he was privileged enough to treat me like shit and just move on like I never really mattered. No matter how many confessions of love I shot his way with Cupid's arrow nothing ever worked. But still I pushed and some days he would give me a little. Other days he would take all of me. My love, my money, my body. He took it all with no receipts or thank you notes to prove we ever existed.

When The Narcissist and I broke it off he said, "Why don't you be you and I'll be me?" We were becoming something else and I knew I needed to walk away, but I couldn't. He would push and I would cling tighter to the idea of us. I knew we could work it out. I wanted it so badly that I lost sight of who I was and what I really wanted. I blame it on my youth and young unrealistic ideas on what a real relationship should and look like on the inside.

See, here is the thing about falling in love for the first time: it's good when it's good and bad when it's really bad. I was truly, madly, blindly in love. Sometimes it all gets a little too much. Everyone gave me advice about leaving him. I was just supposed to let the ashes fall and forget about him. I was just supposed to pretend my heart was entangled in a wicked web the narcissist had created to keep me trapped in his mind games.

You know what hurt the most? When we met years later he denied ever being in a relationship with me. He told his new fling that I was a crazy bitch. We were together for two years and all he ever gave me was a label. The only thing I ever did that was crazy was falling in love with a narcissist.

I realise that love brings you flowers then it brings you coffins. Under the waves I found the strength to wash myself clean. I cried enough to filled a thousand oceans. Love sinks and hope floats. I woke up one day and realized that everything we needed I didn't need anymore. I needed to find my strength to say enough hurt is enough. So I left. I walked away. I packed my bags and moved over 800 miles south to heal my heart. I moved where he couldn't touch my soul any longer.

I prayed and told myself that I couldn't give up on myself. This first heartbreak wasn't life-ending. I just needed to find myself and realize my worth. I didn't want the back and forth, hating him and loving him. He made it super hard to let him go. I hated myself for wanting him so desperately. I know I controlled my thoughts. When the love and trust left me, I felt horrible. But then I realized that this relationship taught me that I'm alive to survive this hurt.

The Narcissist didn't give a damn about me. He looked at other women while he was with me. How is it I never noticed his disrespect? How is it I never saw he was slowly killing me?

Ten years later we met one last time after we broke it off and it tore me up. I tried to hold on. I tried to make a friendship out of the broken love. I tried to forgive him, but it wasn't enough to make all the things he did to me ok. The truth hurts and lies are worse, but I told him how I felt wholeheartedly. I gave him the truth he didn't deserve. I told him how he hurt me. I explained how he never really loved me, I laid it all out, hugged him and walked away. The Narcissist last words came in the form of a simple soulless text saying, "I'm sorry."

The girl in this story is you and me. We can be a crew and walk away hand-in-hand. I got you. We now know our worth and are determined to live our lives full of value and purpose.

Look Up

Can you see me?

I'm right in front of you.

I'm beautiful!

Right?

Can you feel me?

You're holding on to my heart,

But it's beating away.

Will you catch it?

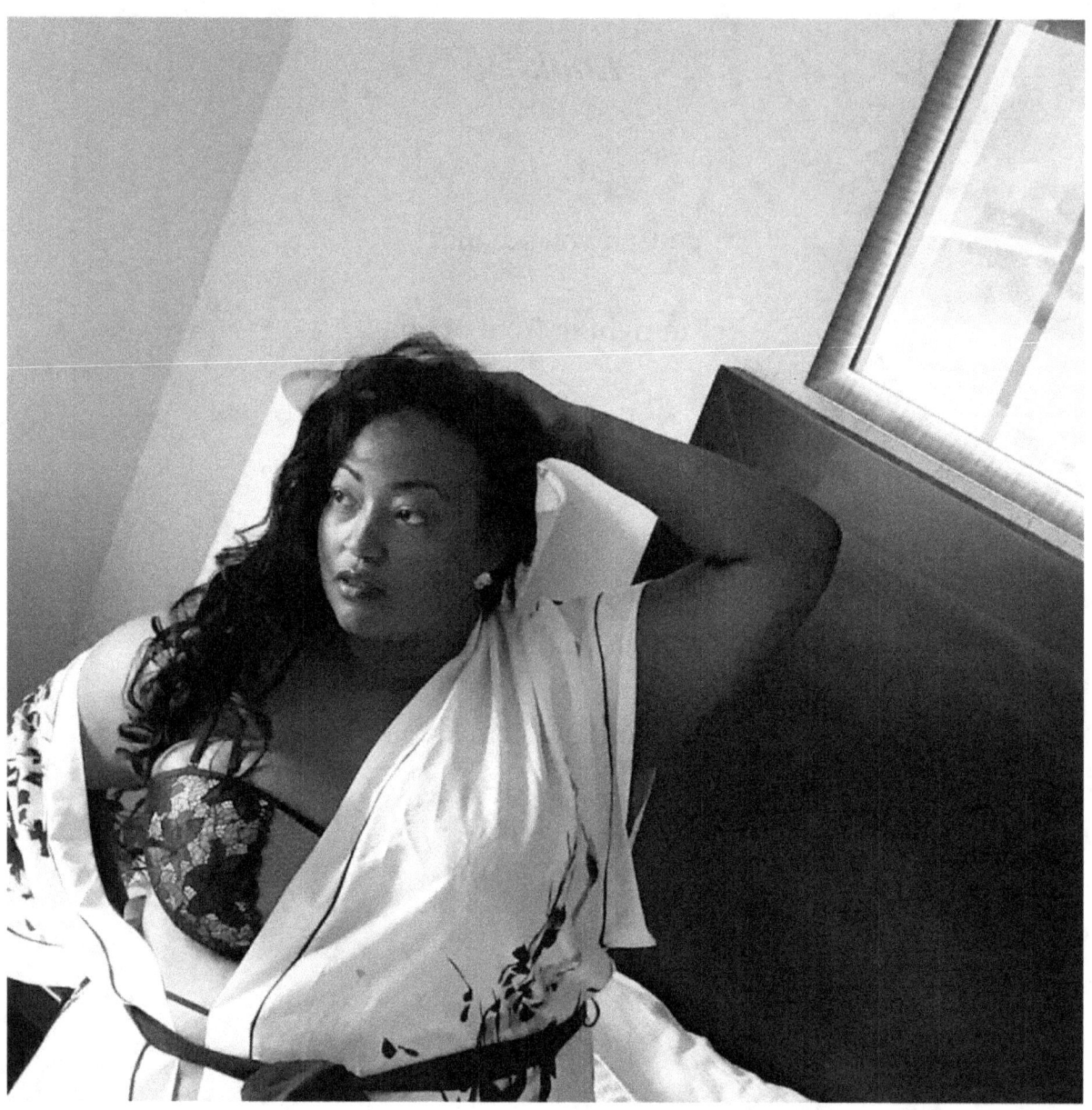

I am a walking
testament to
anyone out there
that with honesty
and self-love
you can feel
whole again.

Kesha Rose Sebert

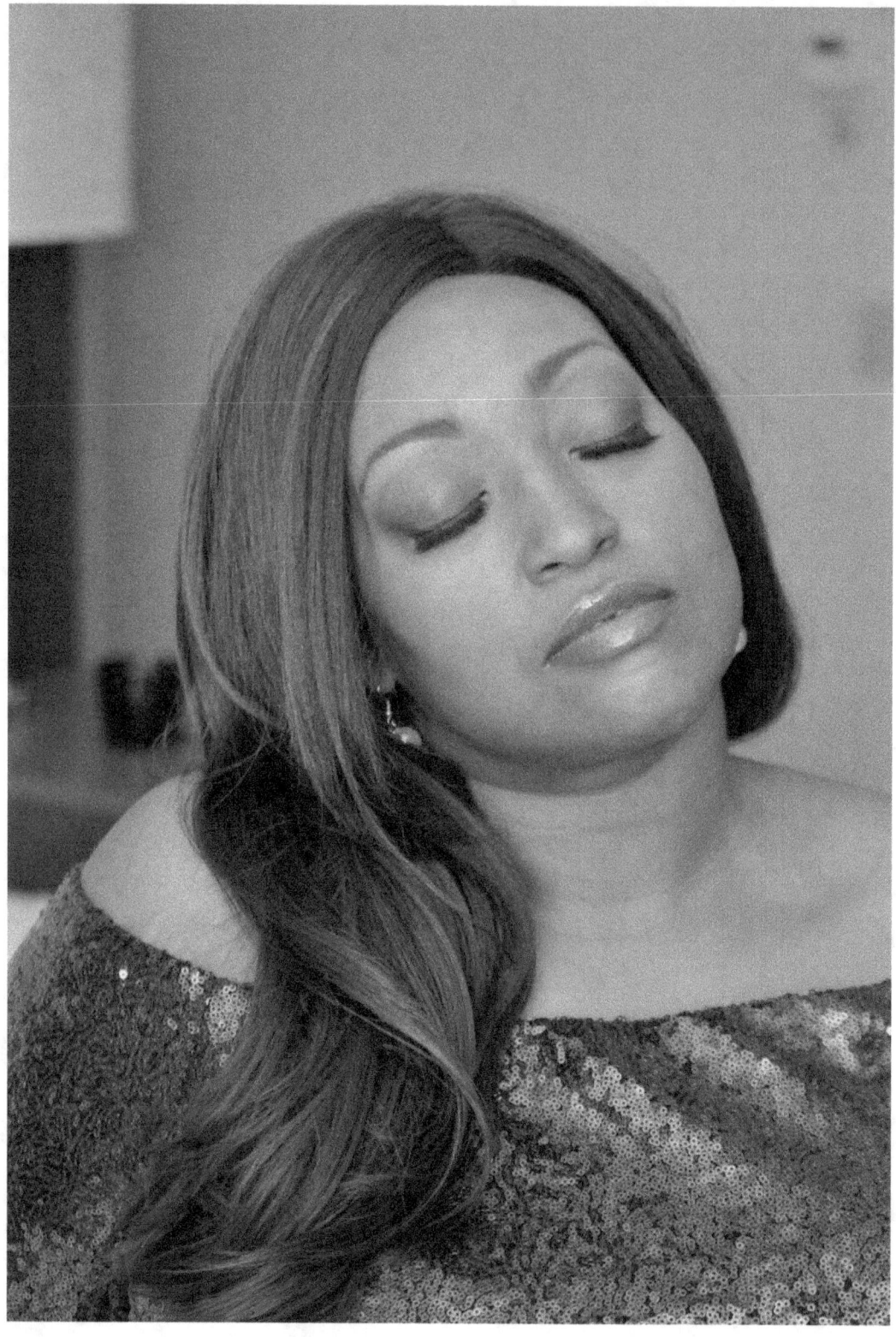

Don't look for it outside. Joy is always in you, all you've got to do is awaken to it.

Roxana Jones

Tell more people that you love them. You never know how much they might need it.

Chris Brogan

Standing in front of a mirror
looking back at the person
you have become is
a very lonely and scary thing.
But everyone must do it.
Every single person should.
It's intimidating and free.

So be free
Get down to it
And love everything about your body.
From your finger to your toes.
Every inch of skin that ever was exposed.
Love all of yourself and the in between part.

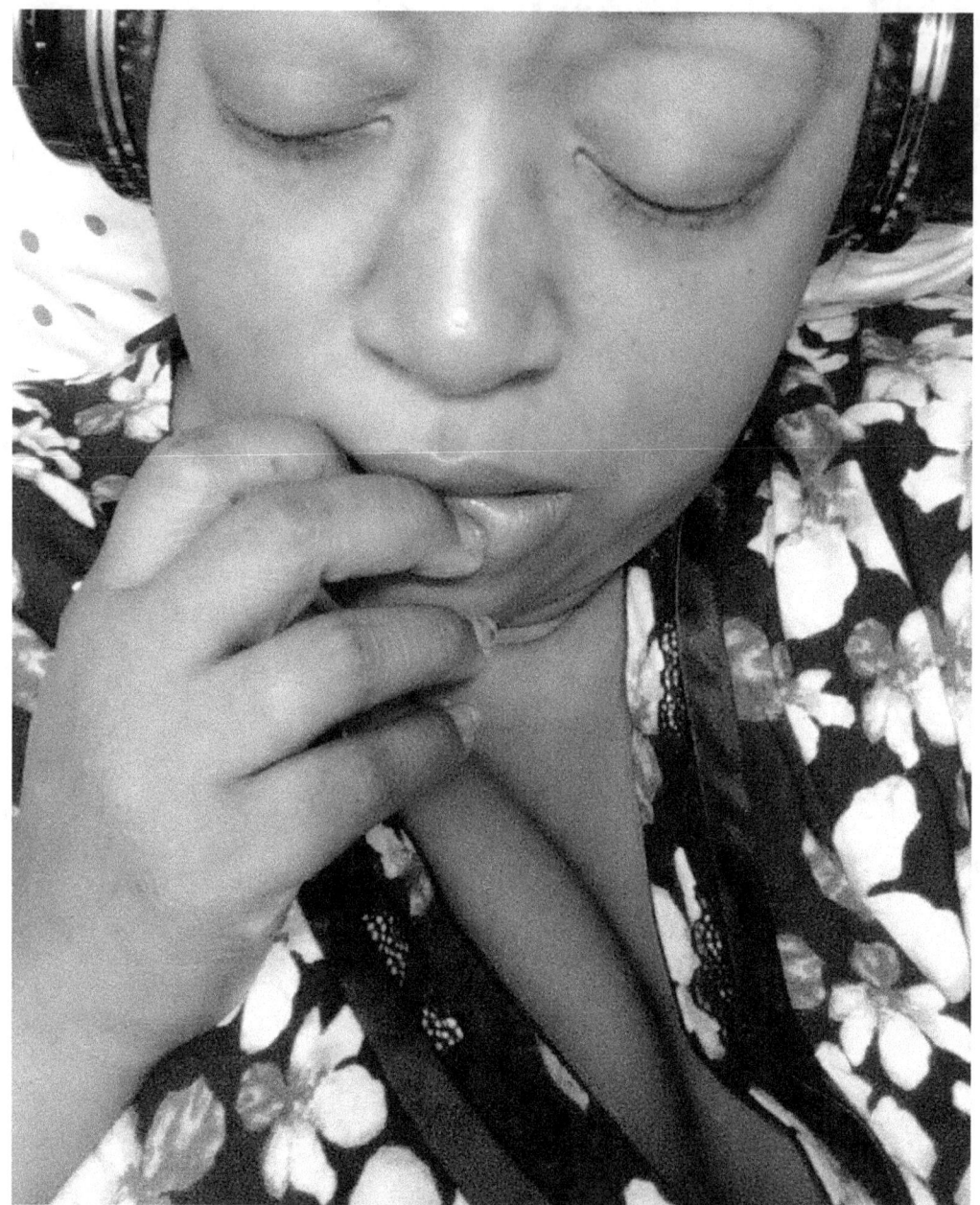

The Fall

We all fall in love once. If we are lucky, then it will happen three or four times. But when you get your passionate soul broken the first time, just know you will mend. Because whoever did the unforgivable and made your heart break, I hope they die a thousand deaths without you in their life. They made the biggest mistake of their lifetime by letting you go. Sorry will never be enough. Recenter and fix hat chi. Focus on loving yourself better than anyone on Earth ever could. Protect your heart. Also remember Karma is a bad bitch.

G.O.A.T

The internet is full of trolls trying to tear you down. Keep climbing the mountain. The trolls will follow in hopes of dragging you down to live under the bridge of hate and despair with them. You keep climbing that mountain. When you reach the top, be the G.O.A.T. you were born to be and tell those who dared to drag you down to crawl back under the rock they came from.

Young and Free

No one owns you.

No one should tell you what to do or say.

When you are dating understand your power.

No one should try to change you.

No one should try and tie you down.

Honestly you are the baddest.

You are and independent passionate creature.

Find someone that lets you be yourself.

Young and free.

Living your life the way you want.

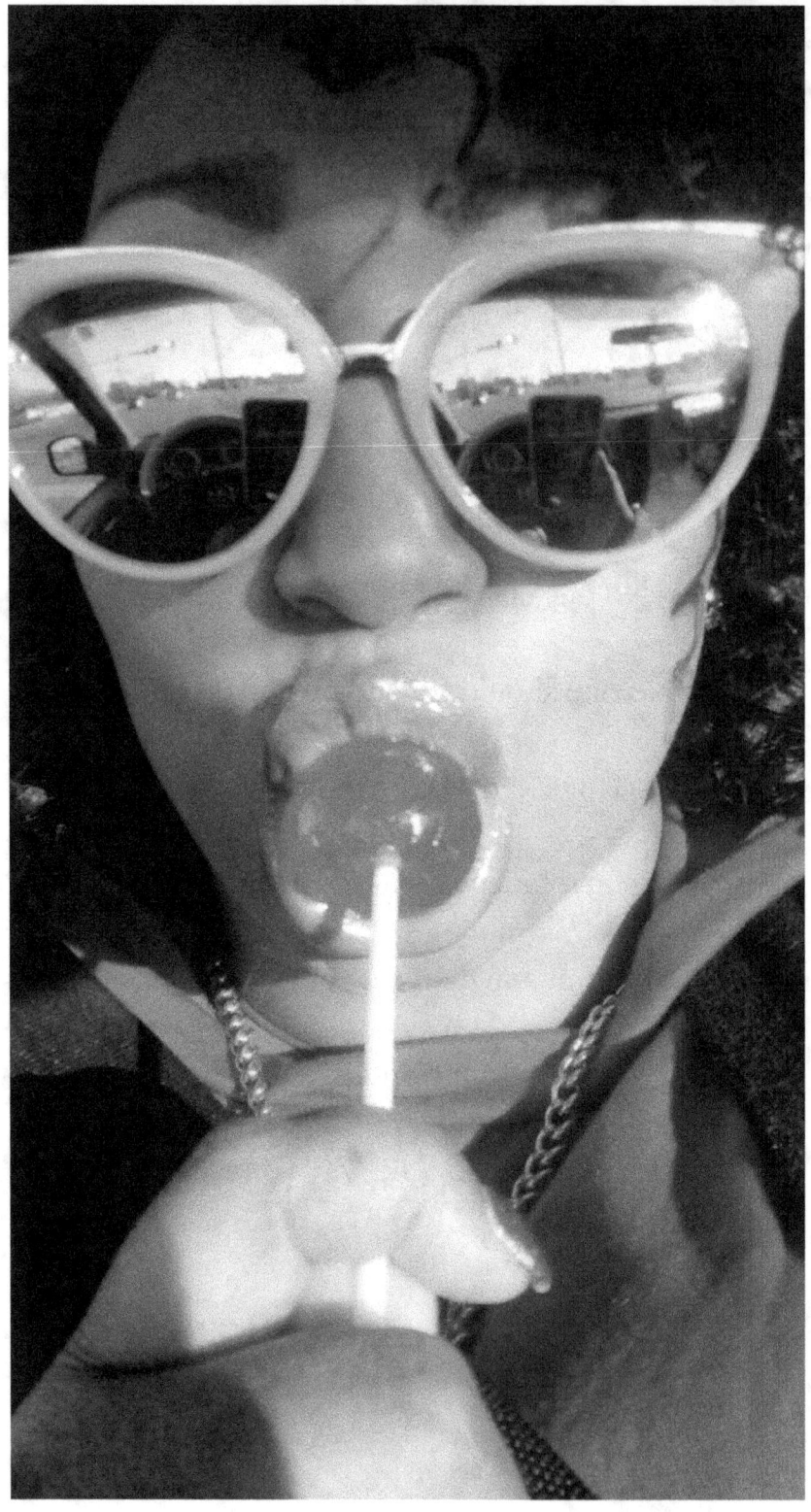

Mirror Mirror

Go unnoticed.

Stay untouched.

It's ok,

In time the right eye will see you shine.

Don't beg for attention.

We are all made the same.

Have hope in your heart.

Even when you sit in the dark,

Know you are beautiful just the way you are.

See your perfect,

Understand you are worth everything.

If you hurt,

Let me be your mirror.

The reflection I will give you will shine greater than Sirius.

You were born with fire and gold in your eyes.

Part II

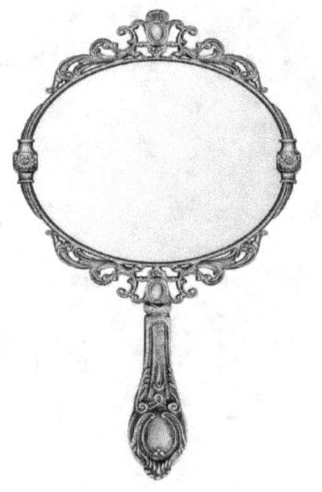

Son premier amour

(First love)

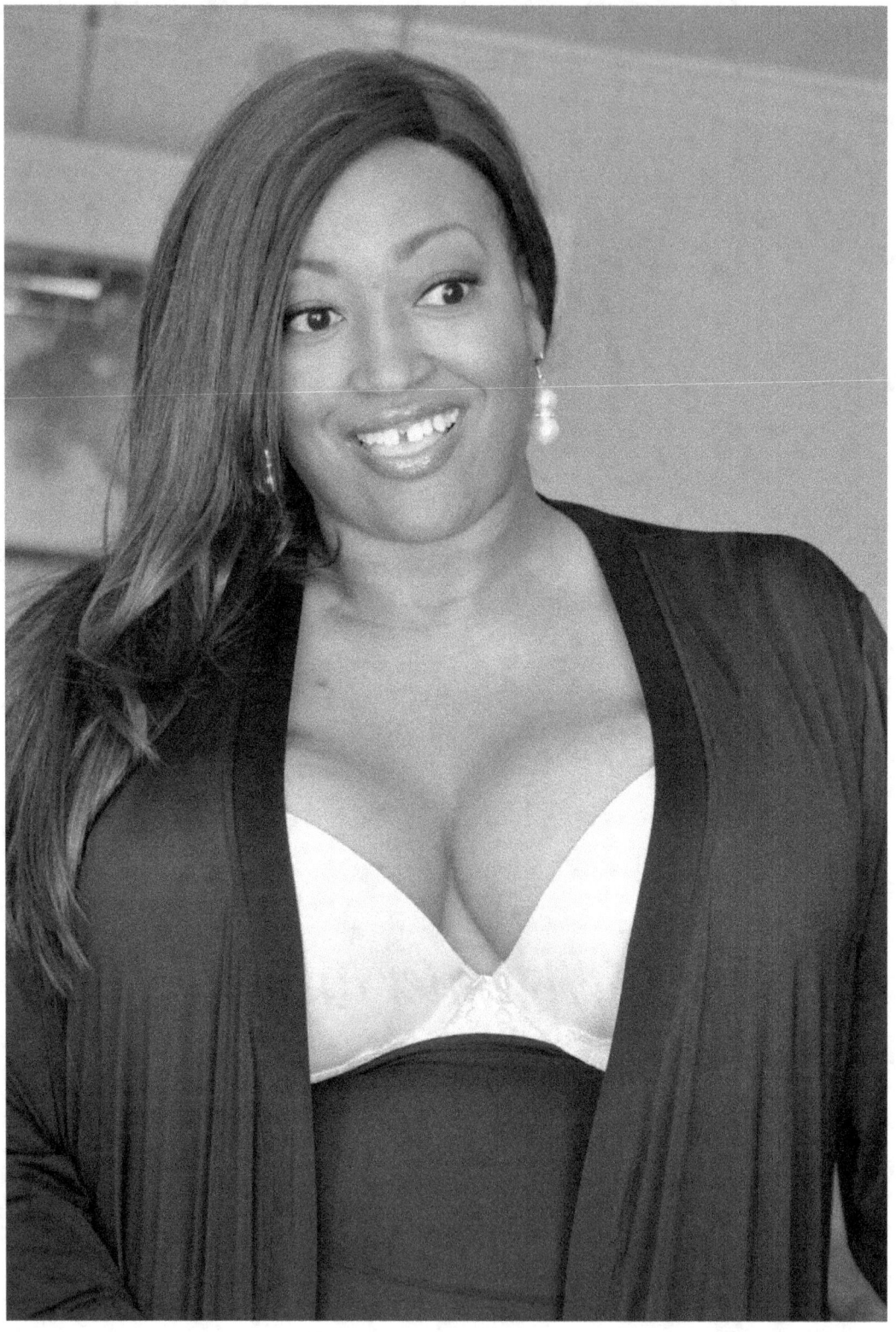

Just Love Me

I love me.

Enough for the both of us.

What are we both afraid of?

You give but you can not take.

I take what you give as it cuts me.

Wake up.

I love me.

I love me.

I love me enough for the both of us.

I don't trust you.

You lie to hide your fear.

You take from my heart.

I let you show me how I'll never be enough.

I love me.

I love me

So I'll keep it 100 with myself.

I want to be with you.

I want you to feel loved and adored.

We are one and the same.

I love you.

I love me.

I love we.

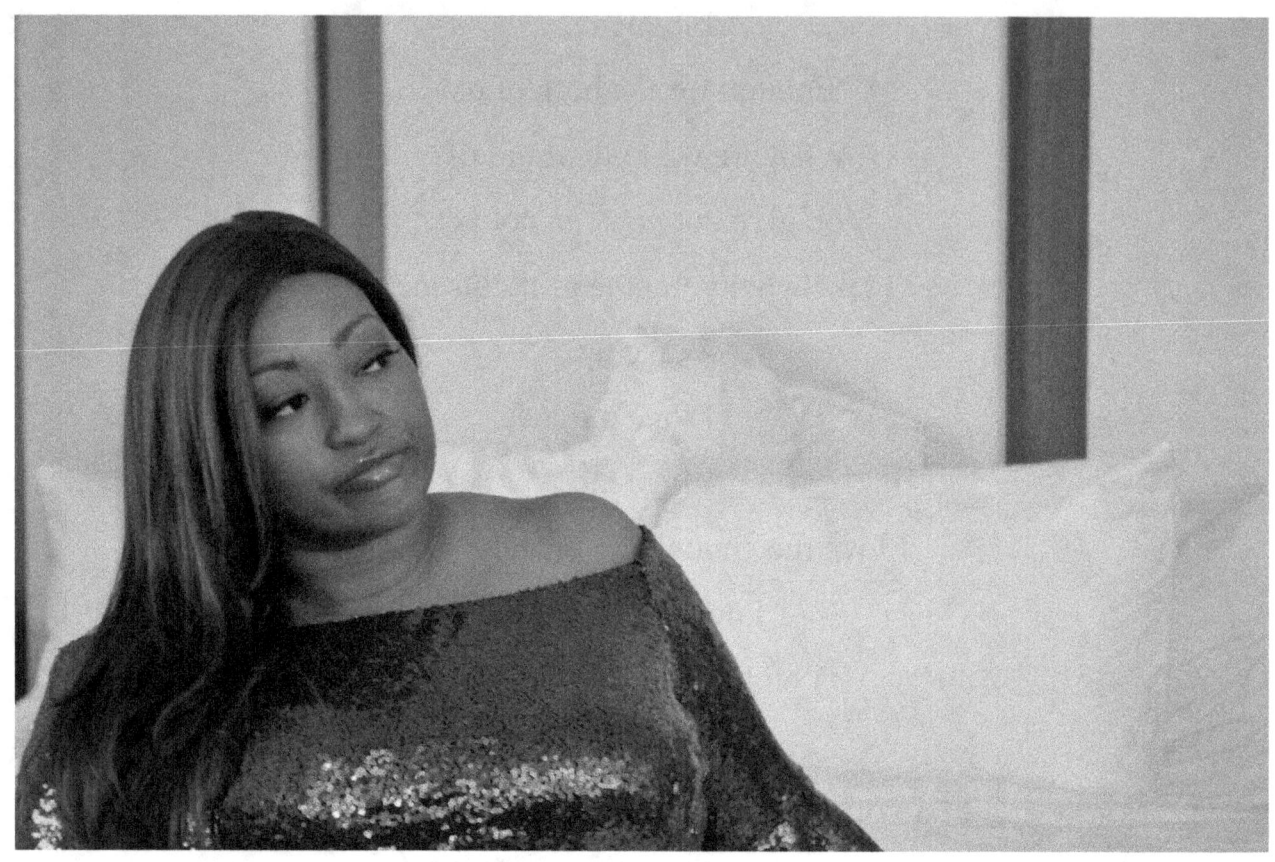

If I Were A Boy

Remember that song by Beyonce when she kept singing about if she were a boy? I think she was on to something. There is a thin line between love and hate we have for ourselves. It's never black and white there is something in the middle. The love and hate we have for ourselves is never simple. It's never wrong or right. So listening to Beyonce belt out those notes got me thinking, if I were a boy how would I treat myself?

Growing up my mother never taught me how to love myself. She was big on making sure my sisters and I were good God-fearing people who loved everyone, but never was the love talk given to us about us. So much advice is given on how to act to attract other people but not enough is given to self-love and respect. Girls are told to look pretty, speak when spoken to and just be good. Be good so boys will like you and you will get married before you turn 25 years old.

Time really moves fast when you hit sixteen. When you hit thirty you start realizing you didn't turn out the way mom and dad wanted you to be. They tried to hide me the world, because they felt it was too big for me. They tried to hide me from the boys in my neighborhood. So for me trying to decide if I was pretty or good enough was the most difficult decision for me. When I hit thirty years old, I felt like I was living in regrets. Regrets that I wasn't good enough for the people around me. I felt my body, face and attitude were trying to find their own place in this world, all the while, I was told to cover up and shut up. This isn't a real way to live for anyone.

There should be more education on being beautiful in your own right. No one needs a degree to help our young women embrace who they are inside and out. We need more people who are willing to be mentors to our young girls and women in order to teach them how to value themselves. Teaching them how to live their best life. Even with mistakes you can pick up the pieces and keep climbing the mountain towards greatness.

We need more lessons on self-love and resilience. There is no magic pill your family doctor can give you to change your chemical composition in order to feel this. We need to rely on the experience and life lessons of those around us. We need to teach our young women how to live, love and laugh more often than not. Because if we don't know the real way to walk in this life being strong and relentless, we will fail ourselves.

If I were a boy, even just for a day, things would be completely different. Inherently more difficult I'm sure, but the way life lessons are presented to me, I think I could understand how to live and love differently.

If I were a boy this would all be different.

Falling

In

Love

I think it's alright.

To fall in love
with yourself.

I think it's alright.

To fall but
never be caught
by someone else.

I think it's alright.
To get lost in love
For the first time.
With yourself.

Martha Cothron

Victimless Hero

The image of a cap

Taped to your back.

The thought of being rescued.

Take care yourself.

Love yourself.

Be the Hero of your own tragedy.

Don't be the victim of your own life.

Love yourself first.

Be your own hero.

Search for what you want.

Don't lose yourself,

loving someone else.

Stand up.

Say what you want.

Don't fuck with karma.

Be the hero.

I honestly think being #beYOUtiful is loving yourself for who you are. Flaws and all. Every day is not always easy and not everyone will accept who you are and who you are becoming. You have to remember to be enough for you and the rest will come. It's taken me a long time to come to the point of being in that frame of mind for me. And I still have my moments like everyone else does. I'm just glad that I've gotten there.

Cristina Ortiz
Sexual Health and Wellness Consultant
with Pure Romance

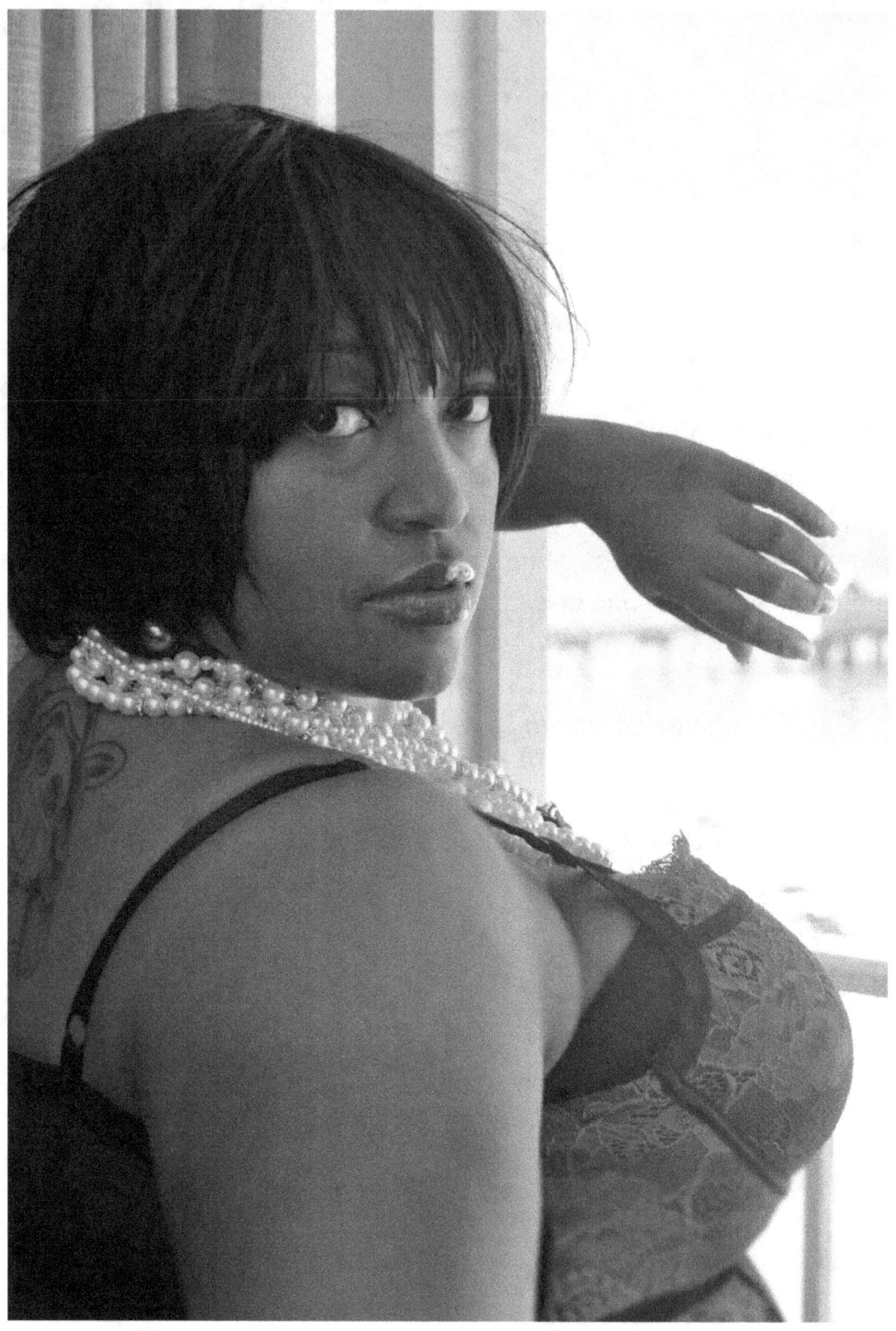

Confident

What's wrong with being

CONFIDENT?

What's wrong with being

PASSIONATE?

What's wrong with being

SELF-RELIANT?

What's wrong with being

YOU?

Part III

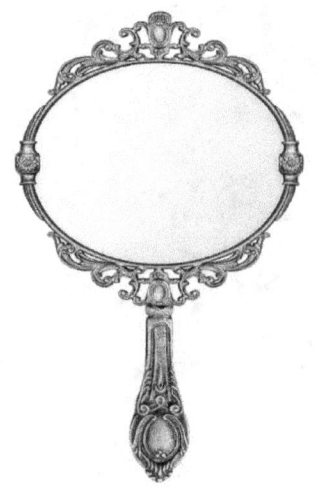

Un triangle amoureux
(Love triangle)

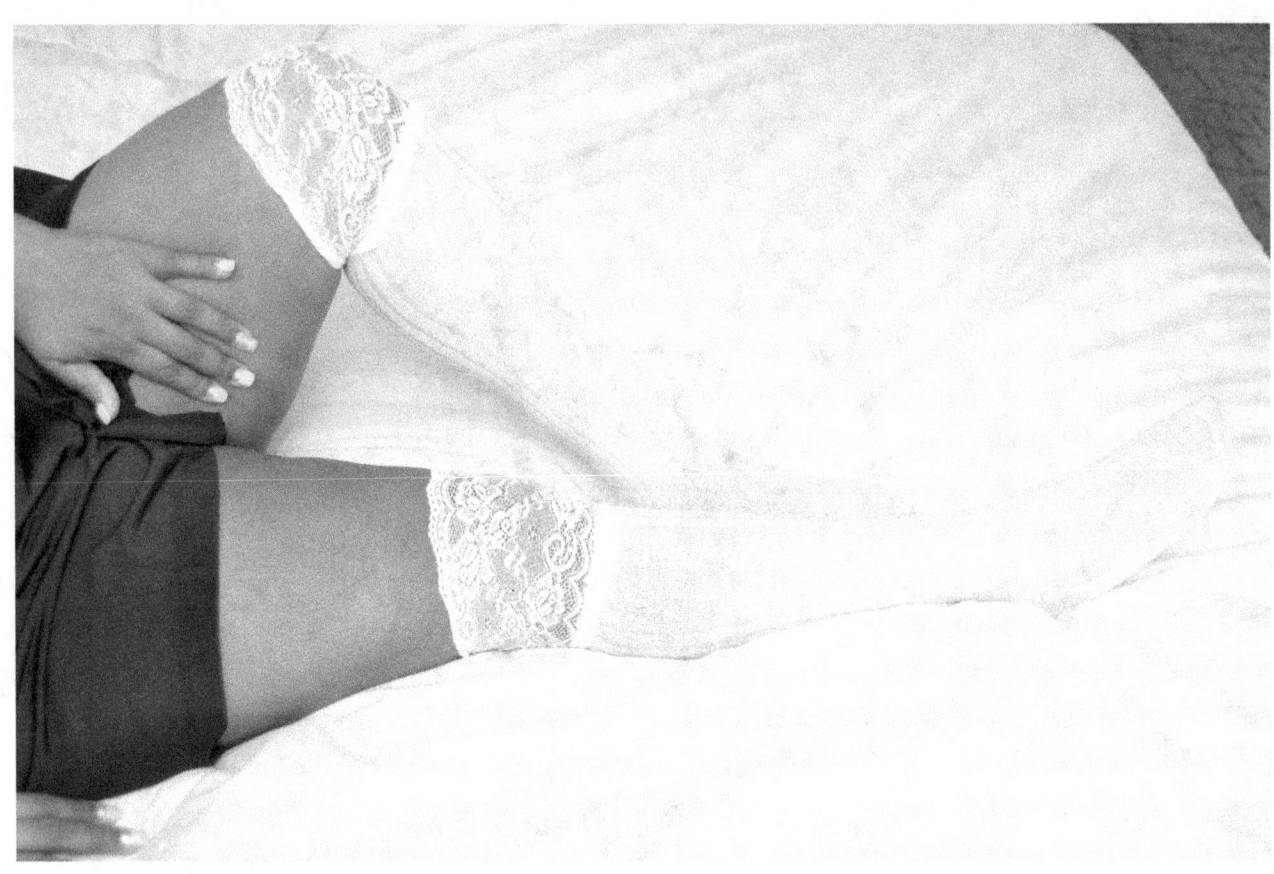

Un

He covered me with sugar coated compliments.
He looks at me he says nothing at all.
His smile makes me feel like I'm the most beautiful girl in the world.

Du

You're amazing just the way you are.
That kiss.
That smile.
This life.
Don't change a thing.

Tois

You're beYOUtiful the way you are on the inside and out.

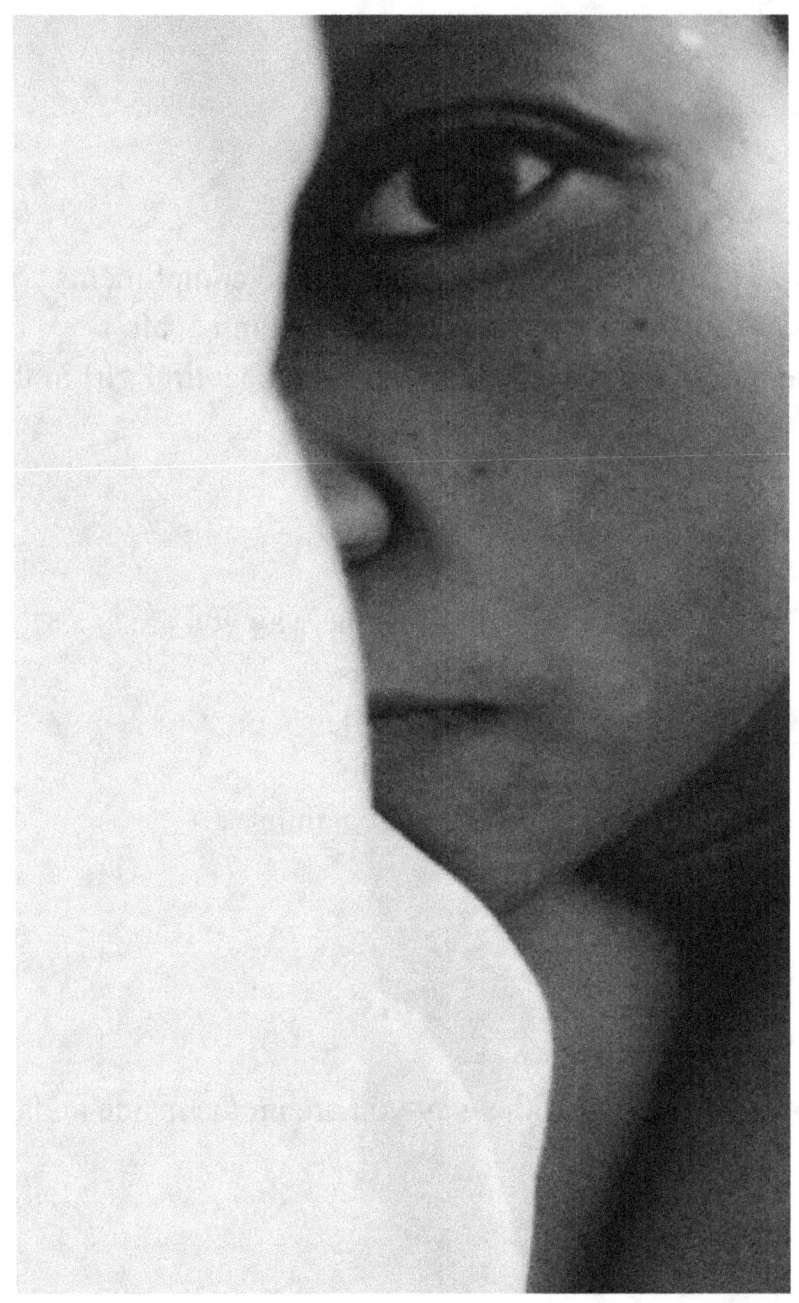

Lose Myself

Something I can't do.

Something you won't do.

Something we shouldn't do.

Lose myself loving someone else.

When the entire time I can be loving myself.

So before I lose myself loving you.

I'll stick with loving me for me.

#TruthTellingTuesday

At some point, you have to make a decision.

Boundaries don't keep other people out.

They fence you in. Life is messy. That's how we're made.

So, you can waste your lives drawing lines.

Or you can live your life crossing them.

Shonda Rhimes (shondaland)

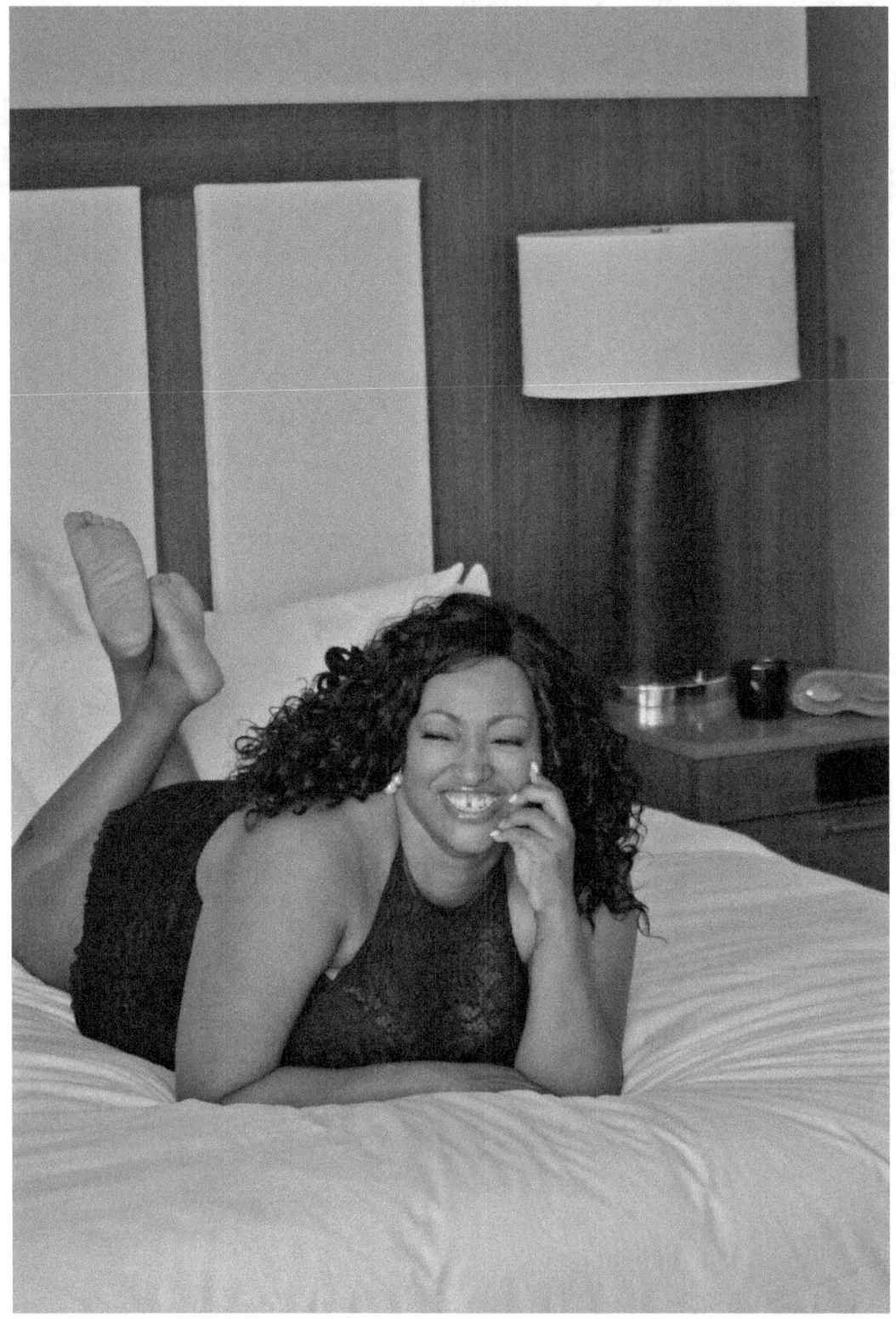

Message

Never let somebody tell you that you aren't beautiful. Promise yourself every day that you will never give up on yourself. No man or woman can own your beauty and hand it back to you on a platter. We all have talents and crafts that make each one of us unique in our own right.

Look back in history that all the woman who paved a way for both you and me to be who we are today. We walk in the light they shine for us to find ourselves and the beauty we have within shines for the next generation of queens to follow. Make them proud. Know your worth and keep shining.

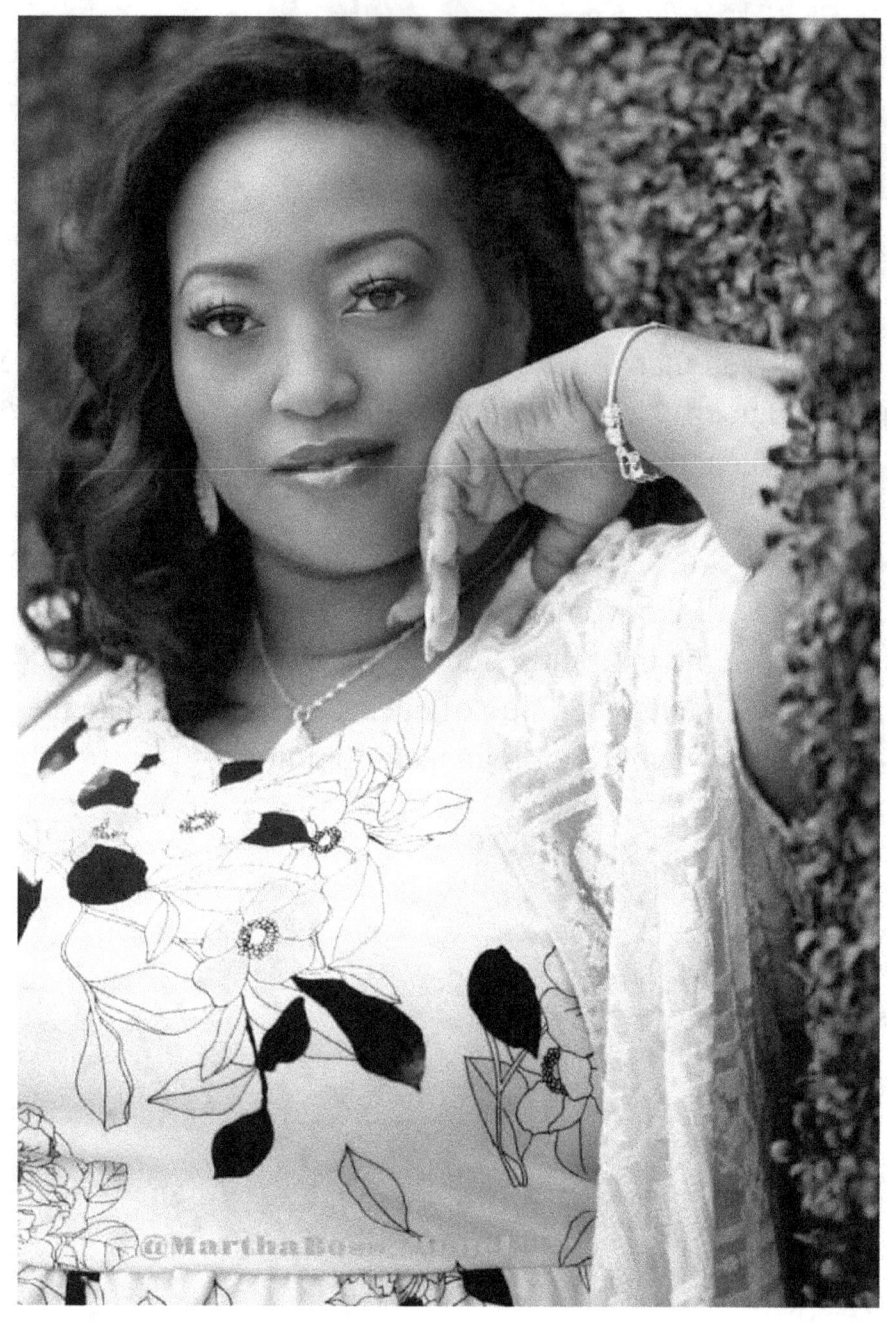

Part IV

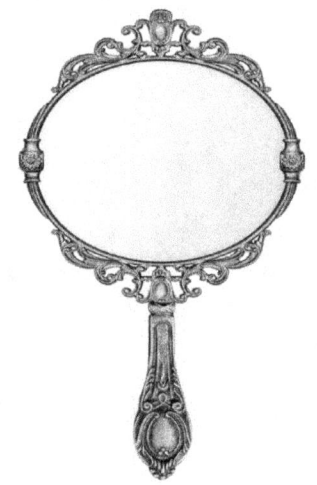

Tu es belle.

(You are beYOUtiful.)

My Mission in life is not merely to survive,
but to thrive; and to do so with some passion,
some compassion, some humor, and some style.

Maya Angelou

Be Happy

My mother never told me I was beautiful. She did tell me that how people see me is all that matters. Their impression of me is what I needed to survive. While i was young I kept climbing for the crown I never thought I deserved. I fixed everything about me. Longer hair. Bigger boobs. All the makeup to cover up that I hated myself inside. Just another stage I had to walk across to be accepted in a world full of beautiful people. Perfection is a disease in our nation. No doctor with a knife can take the pain away or create the person that everyone will love and accept. It hurts to be pretty and perfect. Trying to reach the goal created by people who will never see you.

When you are alone in your room, look in the mirror. Take off the mask you wear for everyone else and ask the young girl or woman staring back at you: are you happy with yourself?

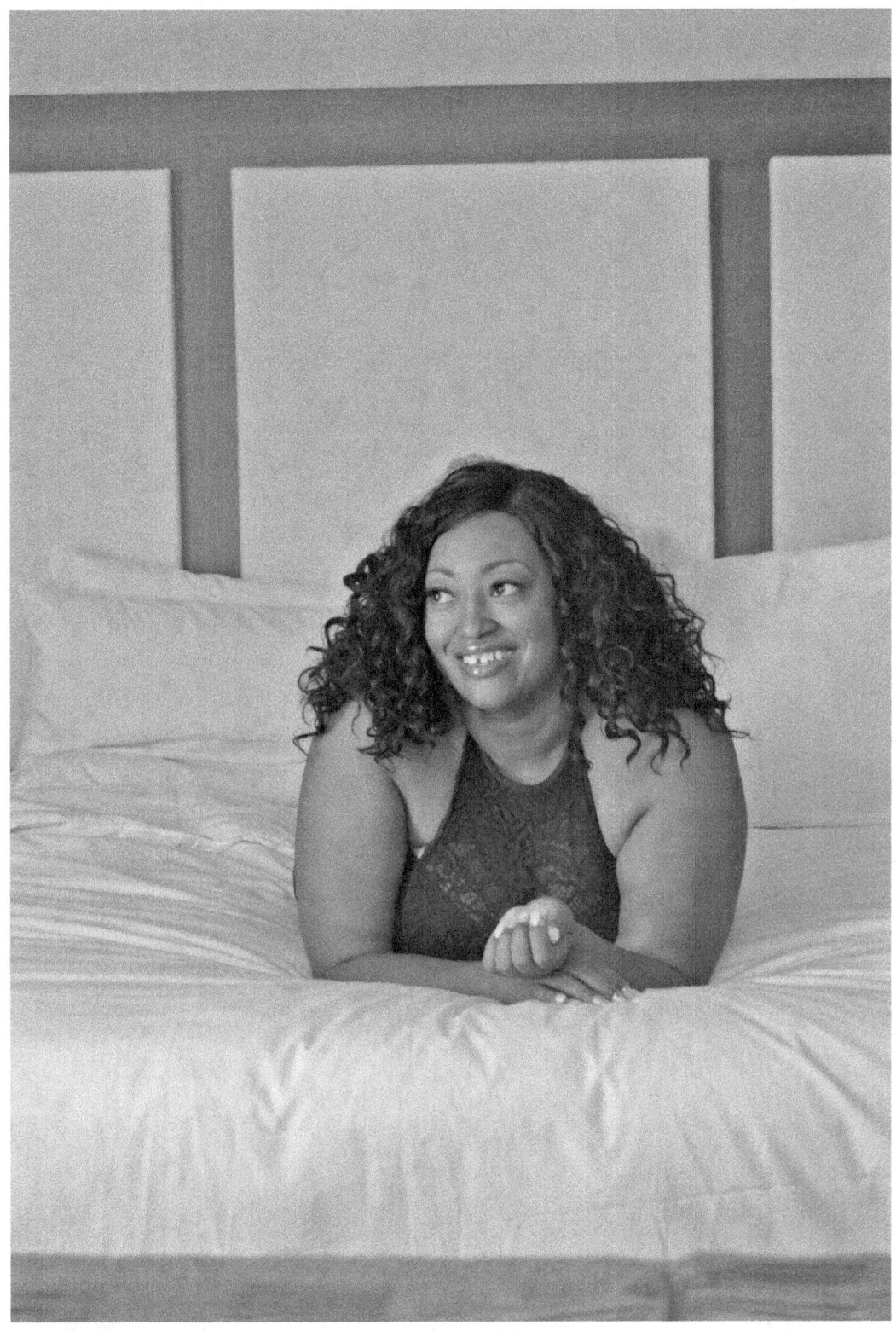

Redemption

I'm searching for the words to say to you.

The words to say to me.

The redeemable words to say we matter.

I'm searching for the words to say to me right now.

The words to say to us.

The redemption to let you know how beautiful we are.

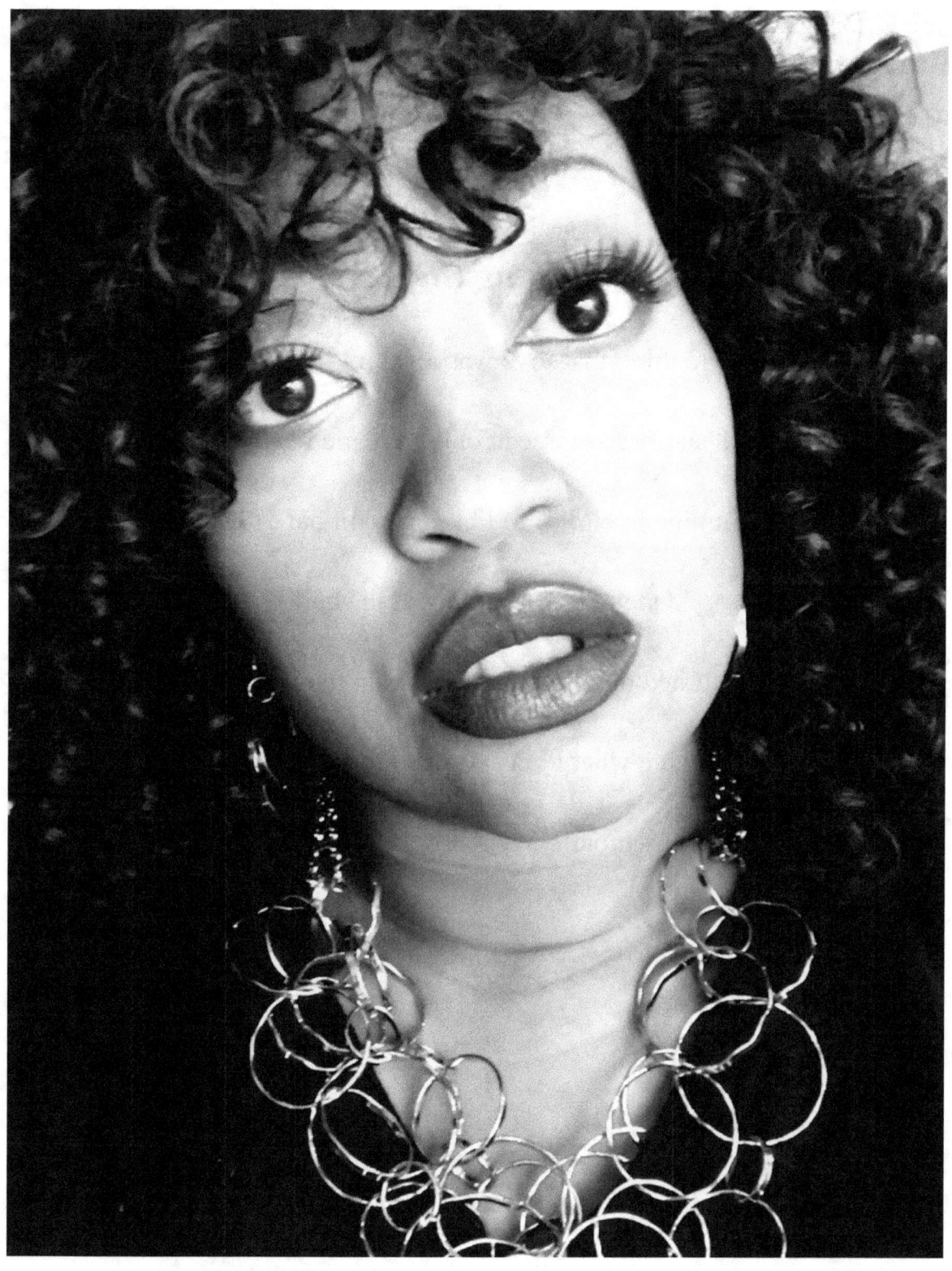

Thoughtless

I use to think that love was a stupid fickle thing.

That my mother can only love me for me.

Running in circles of lies coated in dark love.

One night stumbling in the dark

I turned the light one, looked in the mirror

Seeing what I was always meant to see.

This is my mouth. My Nose. My eyes. My lips.

This is me.

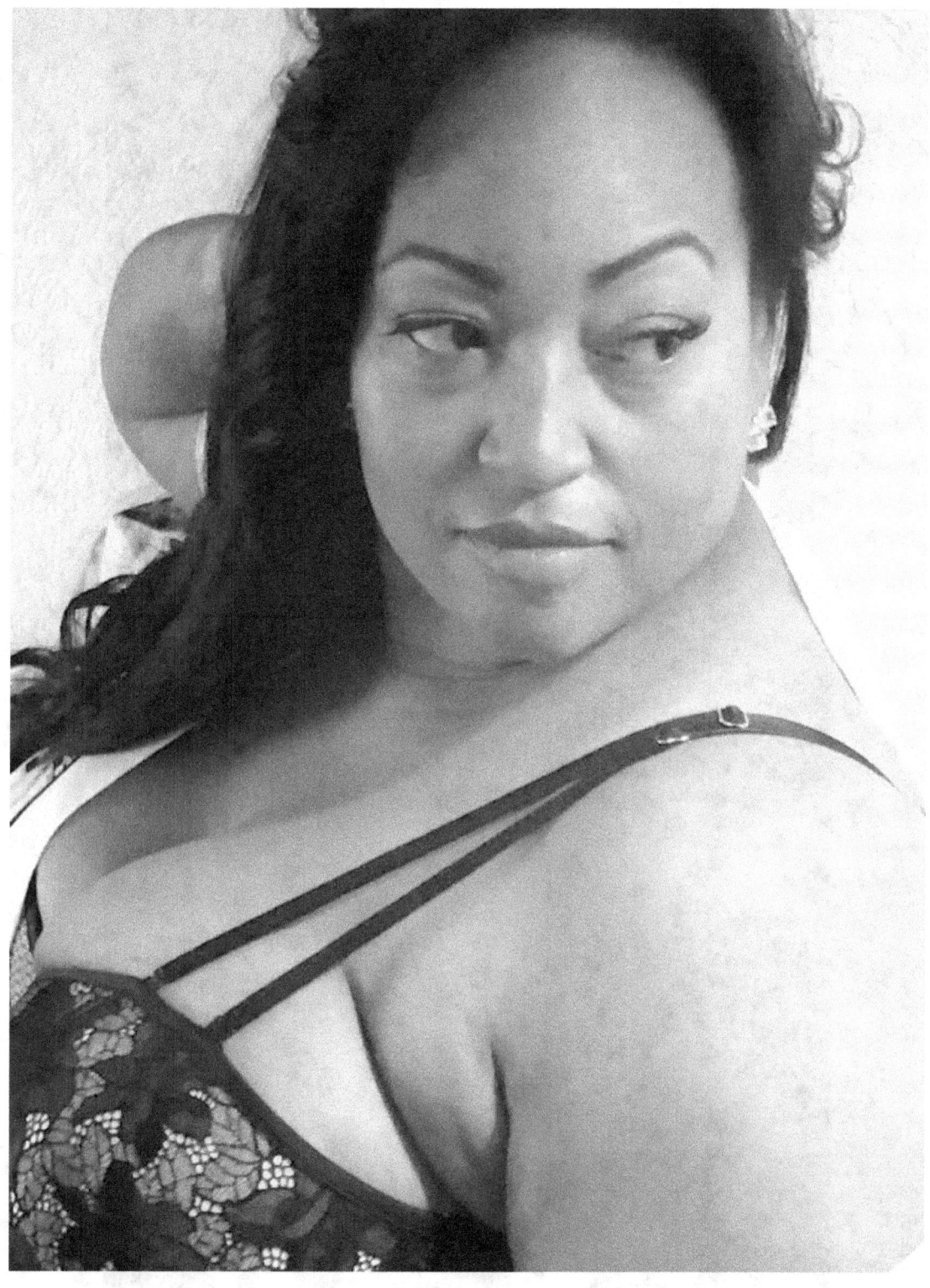

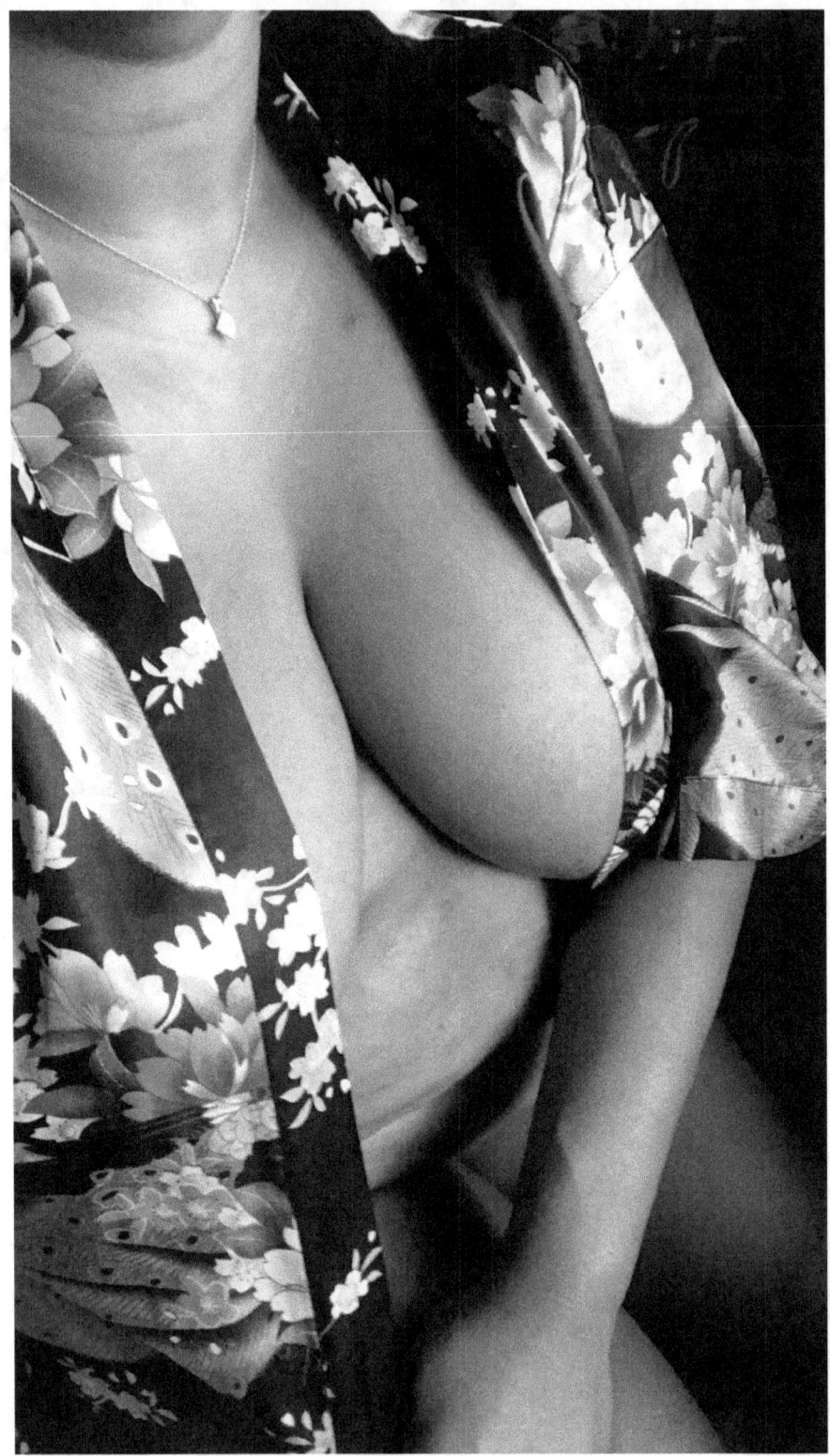

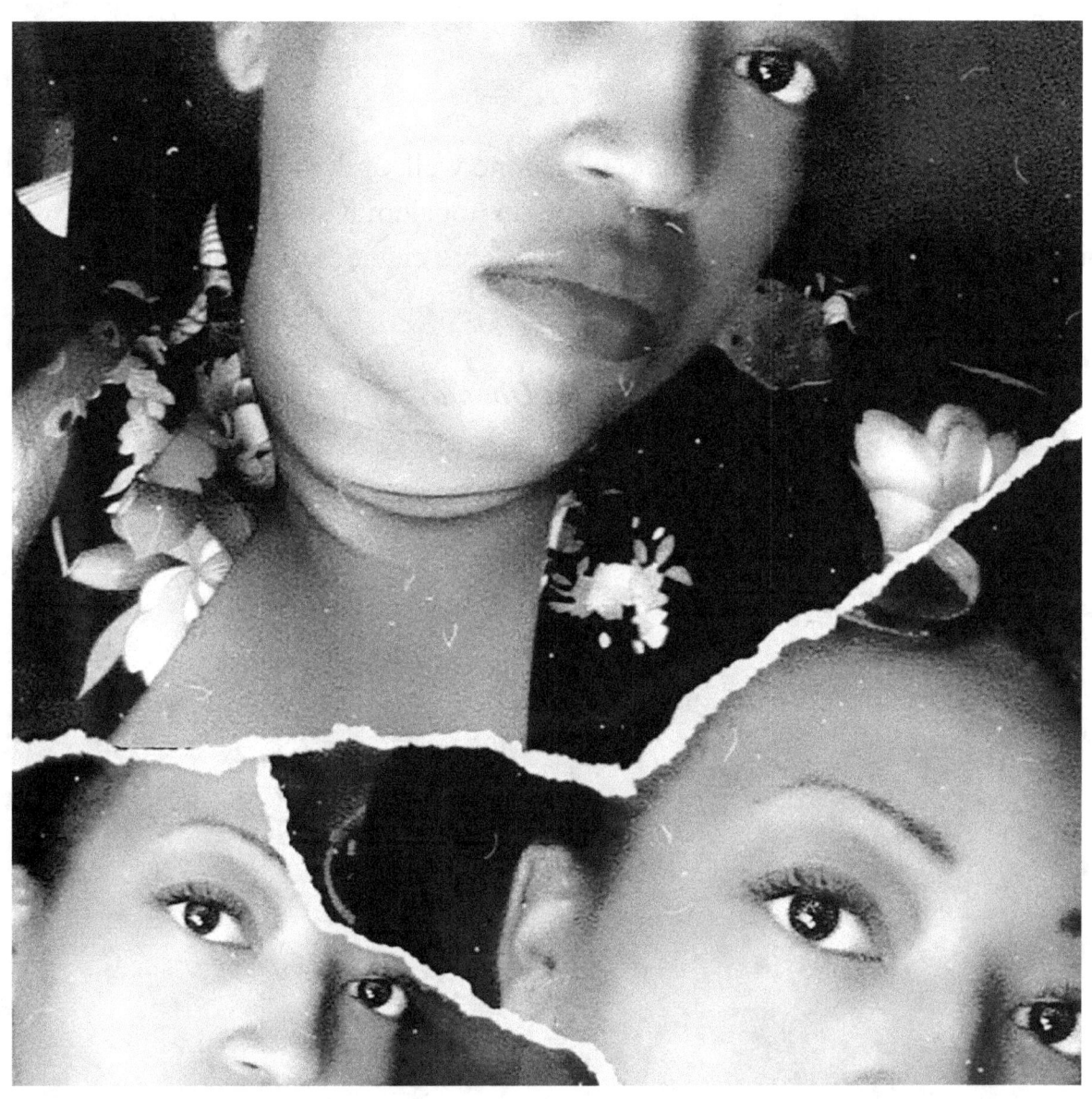

When you've worked hard, and done well, and walked through
that doorway of opportunity, you do not slam it shut behind you.
You reach back and you give other folks the same chances that helped you succeed.

Michelle Obama

Belle

Brazen

Elegant

Lovely

Legendary

Enthralling

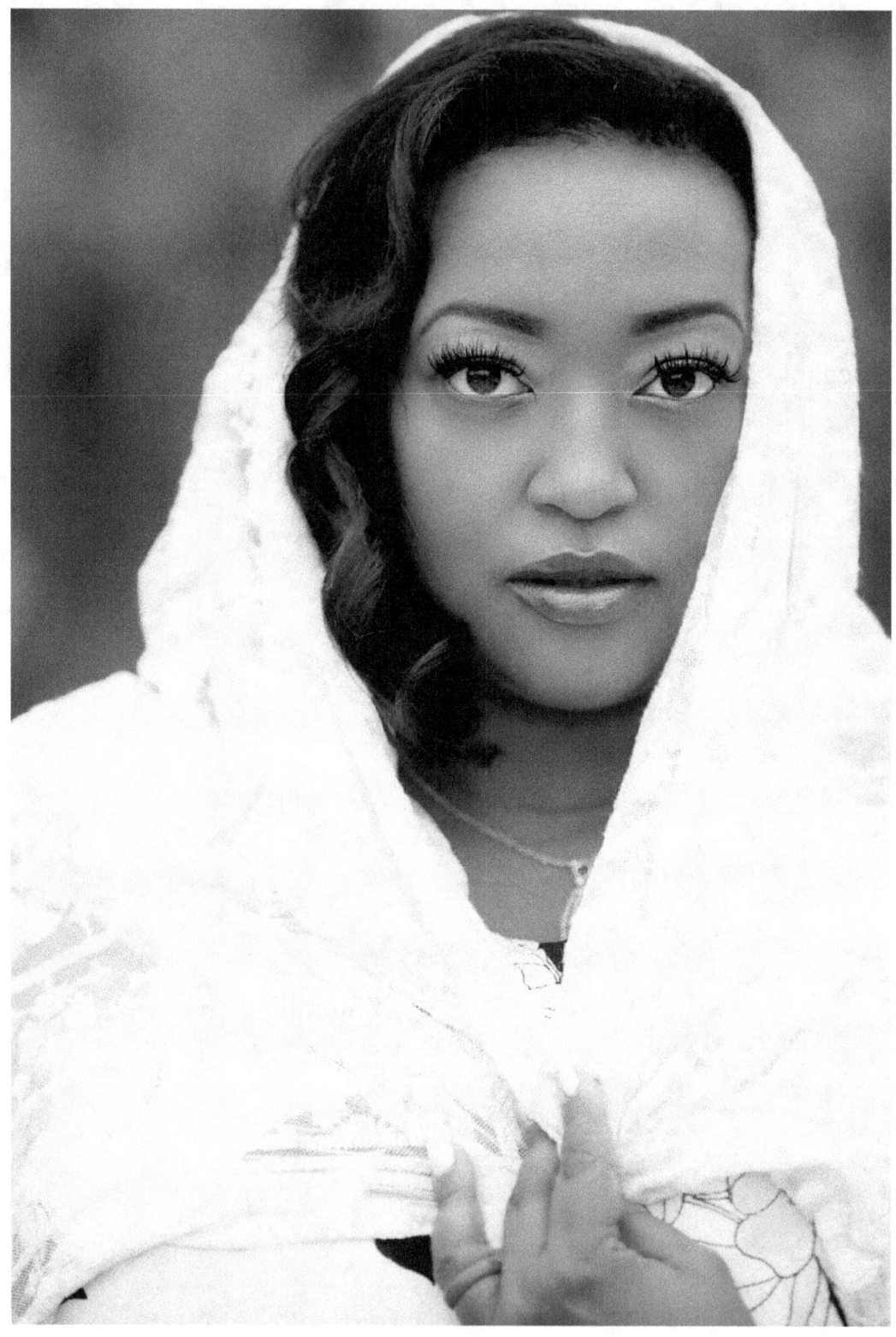

Eyes Wide Open

He will come to you when you least expect it. He will surprise you. He will challenge your faith in love at first sight. You've know him all your life. You sat across from him in Algebra class in high school even though he was three years older than you. You were the nerdy girl and he was the guy too cool for school. He lost touch with you for ten years. You walked back into his life as the friend you always were. He lost you again, but this time you looked for love in other places. You grew in knowing who you are as a woman. Another ten years passed, and you felt as if something from your life was missing. You craved a change. Your prayers to God were specific. And so, the cat came back, and your heart began to beat again. He wants you the way you've always wished he would, but with limits. Your heart wants to know is it now or never?

Queenology

The value of woman isn't in her status in a certain class of people.

It isn't in the numerical value of her bank account.

To be a queen you must be schooled in **queenology**.

Know your **worth** and refuse to give discounts.

Act like a **lady**.

Walk with your head held high as your **standards**.

Know you are beautiful on the inside as you are on the outside.

You you carry yourself as a queen,

They have no choice than to treat you as one.

You were born a queen.

It's in your DNA.

If you were meant be controlled or oppressed

You would have come with a remote.

That's not your life.

It's not the legacy you were meant to build.

Take control of your destiny.

Ignore those who try to discourage you.

Don't give up on your crown.

B. E. Y. O. U.

Be who you are no matter what the crowd screams at your back.
Be the person who is kind and gives love endlessly.

Entertain the fact that you can be whomever you want.
Explain your actions to no one.

You will lose friends.
You will be talked about

Out of darkness comes a light that shines brighter than a thousand suns.
Out of pain comes the feeling of love that is all consuming.

Understand love.
Unfollow the train of self-loathing.

Be You.

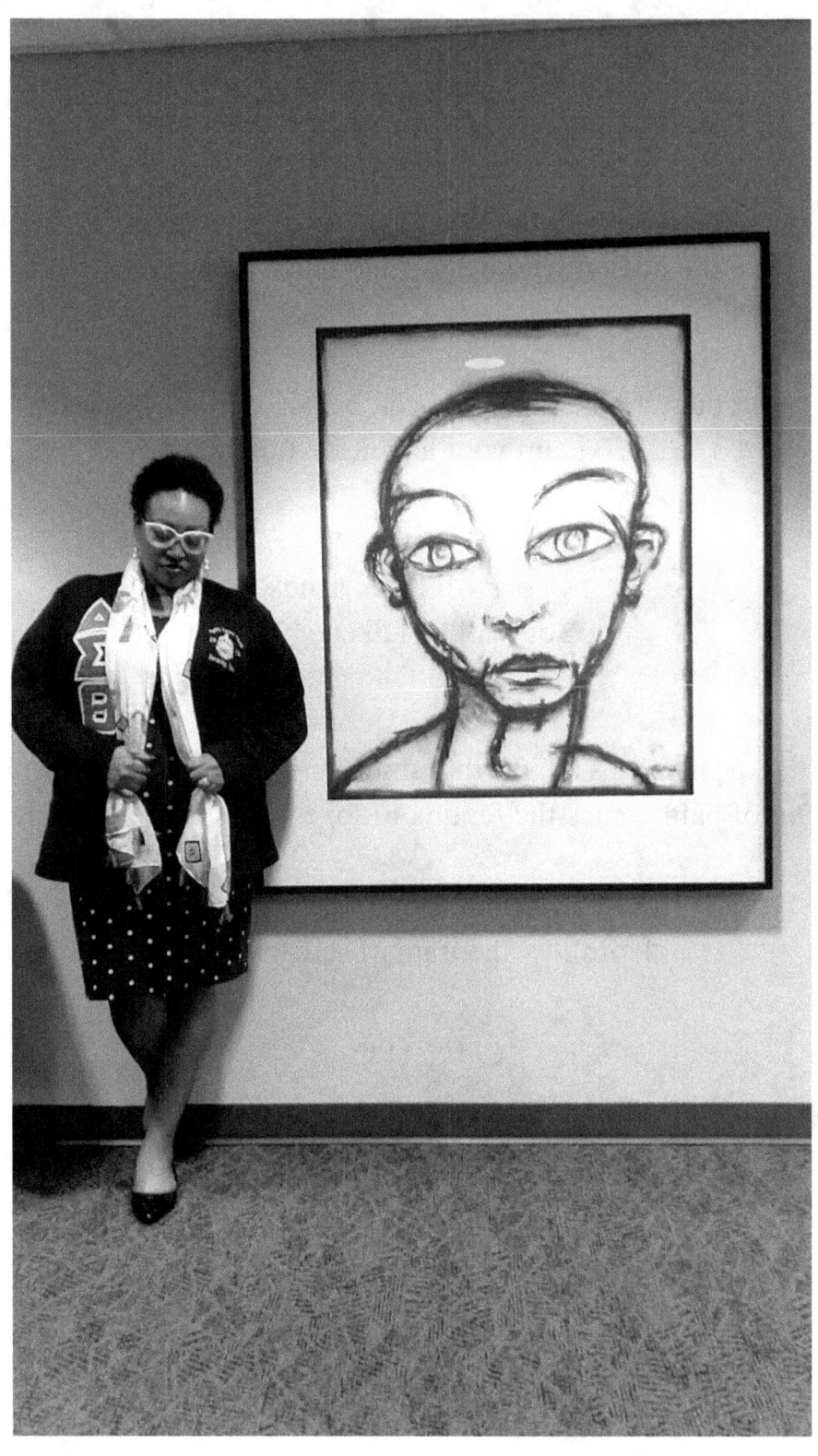

I think the most truly beautiful people are the people who've managed to connect inwardly to themselves, not in a cliché "love yourself for who you are" kind of way, because I think it's a lot to expect of any human to consistently feel a sense of affection and serenity for themselves. But the people who still engage with their own inward lives, who are actively working on becoming smarter or more spiritual or more genuine or simply more *themselves*, these are the people we are drawn to, as if by a magnet.

Sierra Simone,
author of the 'Markham Hall' series
and the 'New Camelot' Series

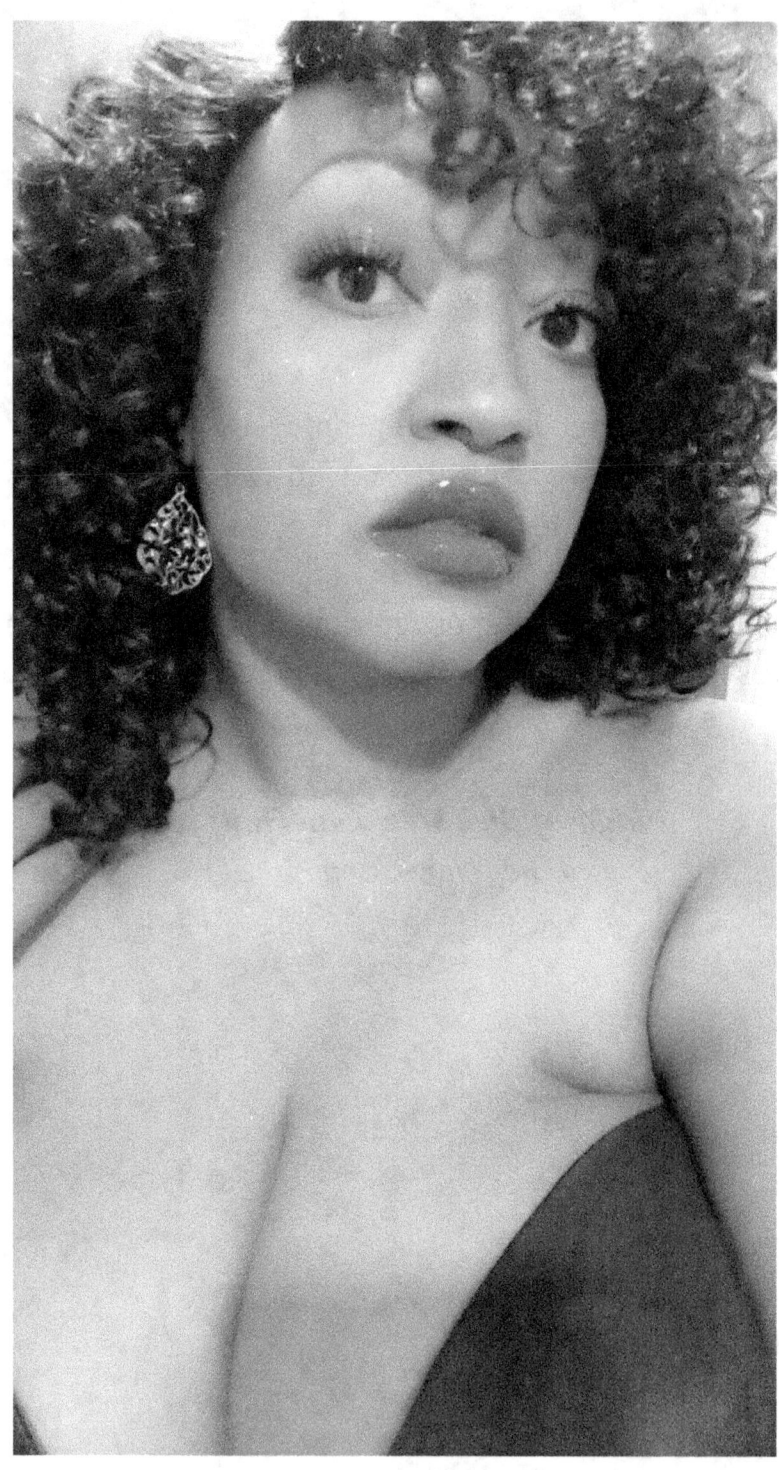

First you GROW up, then you GLOW up.

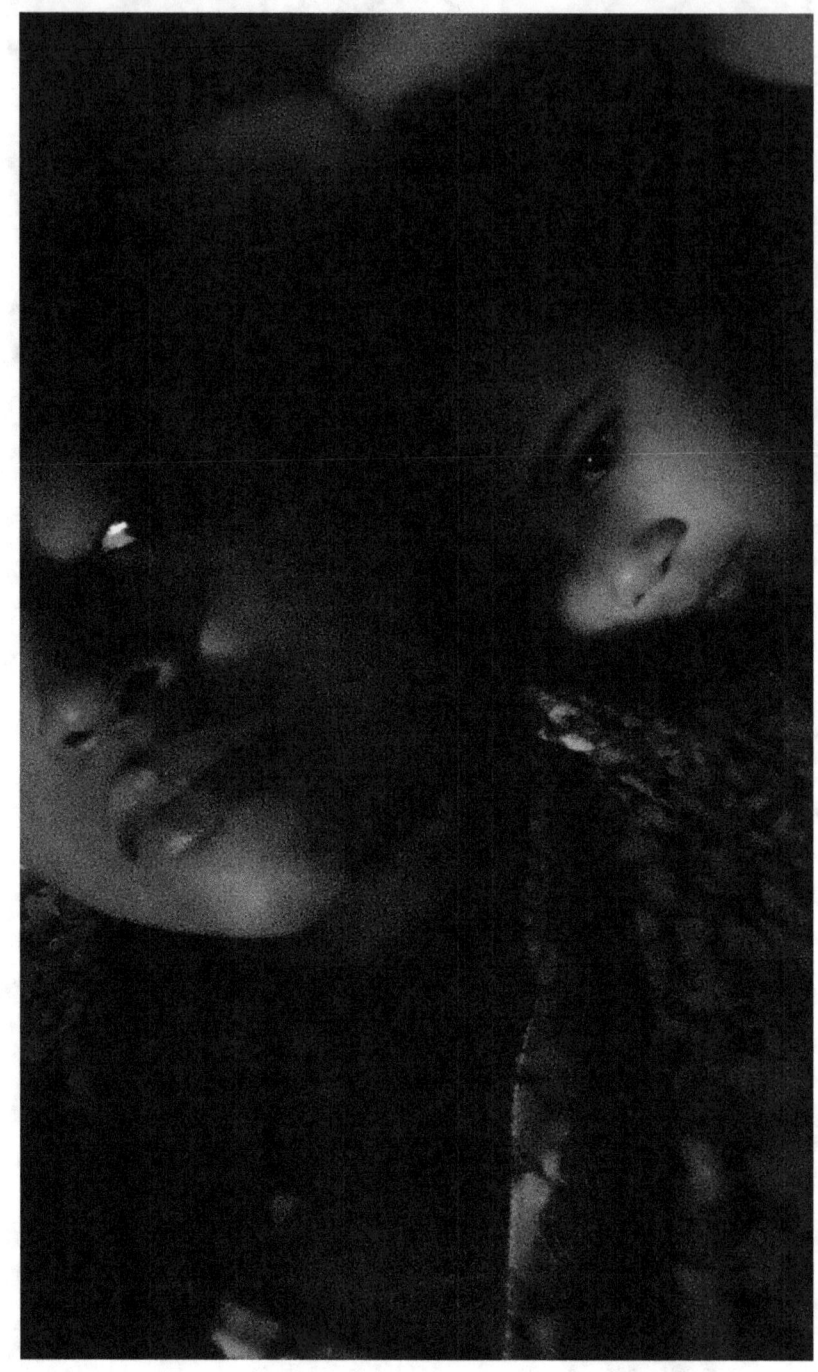

True beauty is found through love. Love is the central most important component in beauty because it's self love that makes us feel beautiful and it's love of others (or love of their esthetic) that makes us see them as beautiful. Love is the foundation of beauty. Confidence is the means in which it grows.

Danielle Allen
Author of 'Disasters In Dating'

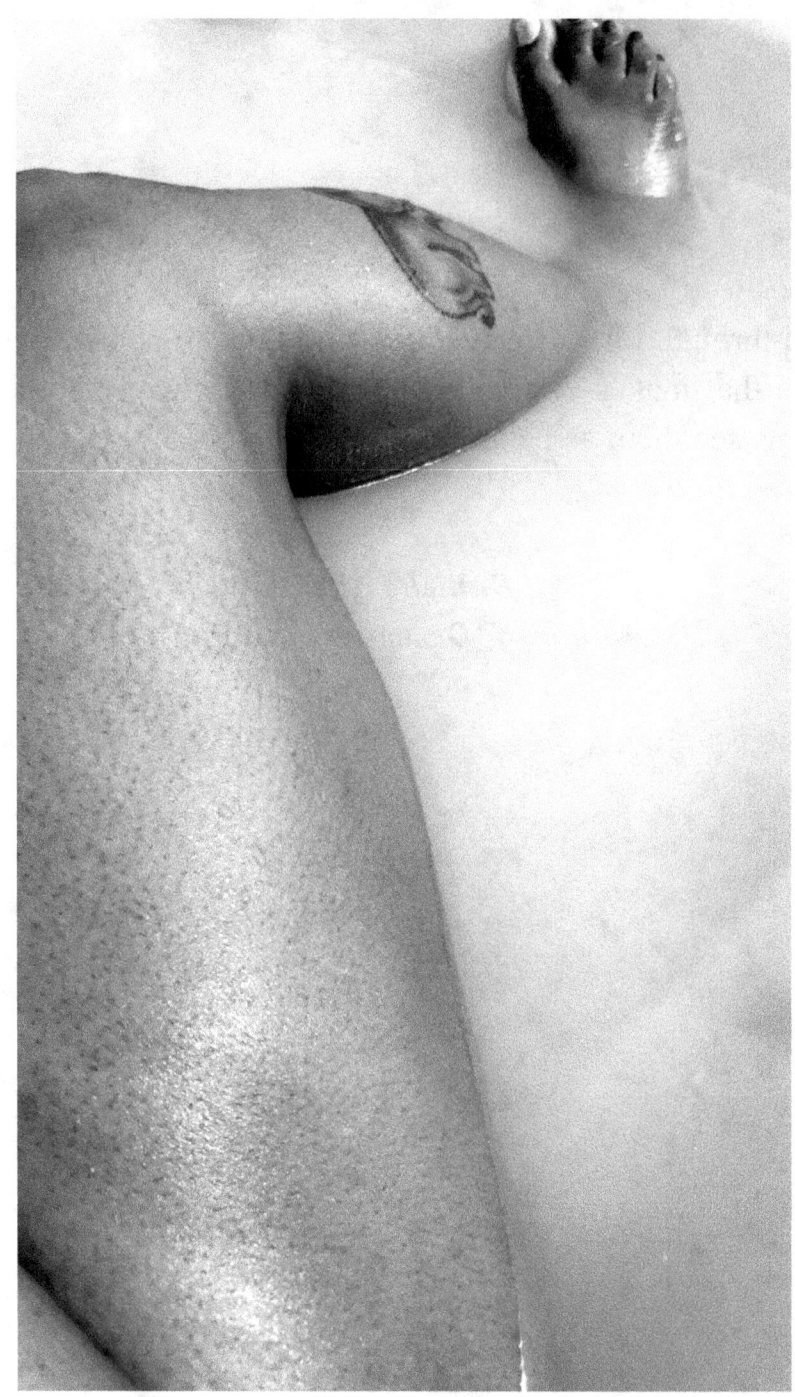

If I teach you anything let it be this my dear:

When you've given up, look up to sky.

When your friends have all left you behind, turn your eyes up.

When every song on the radio makes you feel sad and lonely, feel me in your heart.

Never look down when you're walking.
Smile when you look in the mirror.
Close your eyes when you look up at the sun.
Never give up.
Believe in life after life.
Be strong enough to value yourself more than you value a quick buck.
Work it.
Never let them see you down.
Smile while you hurting.
Even when you have a shit day, know you are still killin' it.

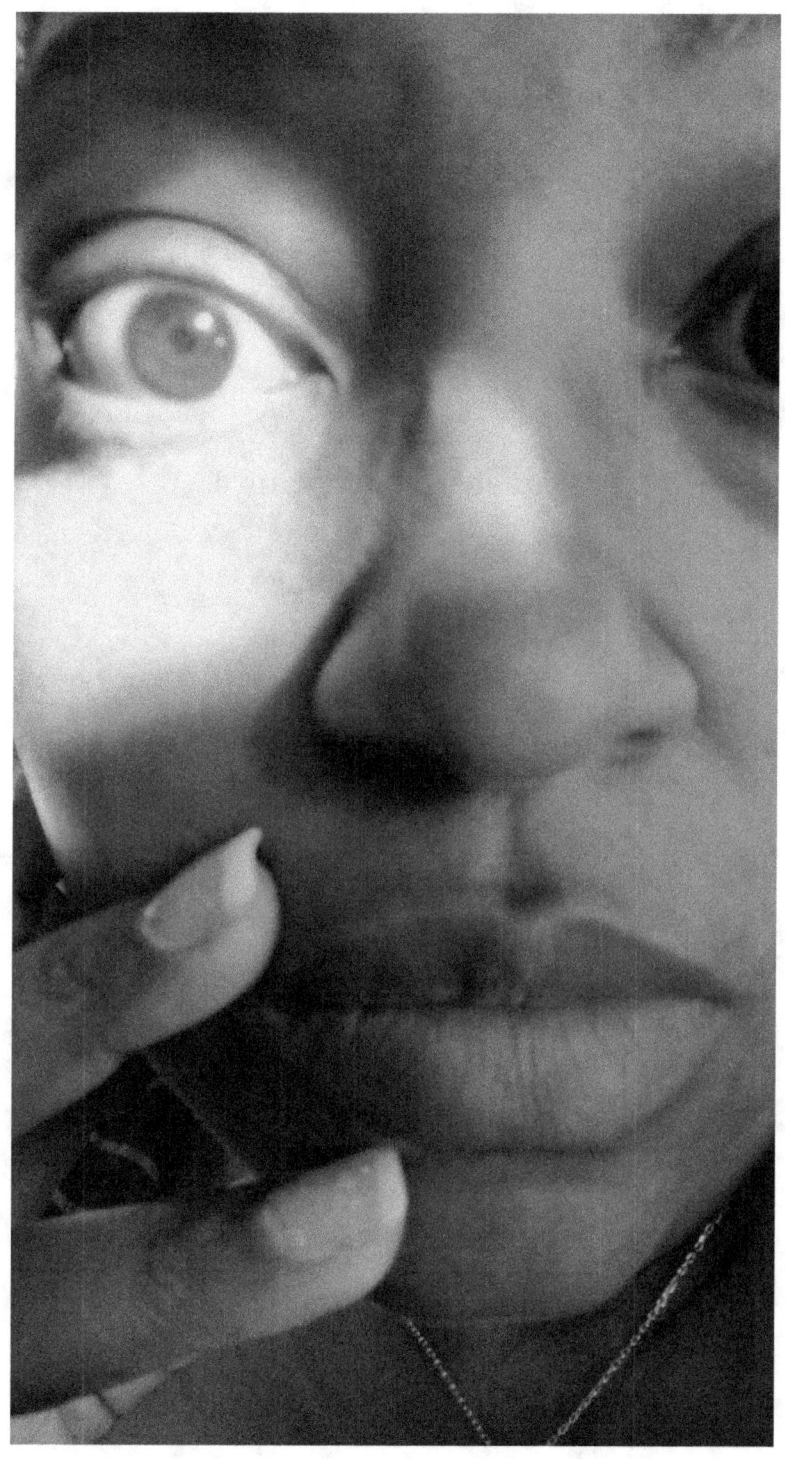

BO$$

Work ahead of the crowd.

Break glass ceilings.

Be confident

Use common sense

Be BO$$

Pledge allegiance to your independence.

When I Grow Up

When I was seven, I knew I wanted to be famous. I knew I was destined to be something greater than the four-eyed girl with pink coke bottle glasses and a love for white boys. Be careful what you wish for because you just might get it. I wanted to be a star and in movies. I had to be on TV and be seen. Driving a nice care with a huge house that I would live in by myself.

When I was fourteen, I learned the hard way that all people say what they think we want to hear. That lasts until you can no longer afford to buy their affections.

When I was twenty-one I promised myself, I would find my prince charming and convince him to marry me because I could sing and give him forehead kisses. I was looking for someone I could mother, because in reality I missed mine. The one who abandoned me and the one who raised me.

When I was twenty-eight I fell into the peer pressure that the only true way of happiness was having children. Because when you are married and not in love it's just what you do. Know what your real job. No one ever told me the struggle I would take to make this happen. Pills, tears, needles, self-loathing, probs, pain and disappointment.

When I was thirty-five I became a hot topic and people talked about me. Not for all the awesome things I've done for my community and children in the foster care system. They saw what they wanted to see. They saw what I tried to make sure I never was. I developed "resting bitch face," which in turn made me an automatic angry black woman by way of societal stereotypes.

Self-love, value, worth, acceptance, joy and want is a battlefield. We stand in our own way at times searching for things that we think we want. As I continue on this journey I still say be careful what you wish for. It's hard to prepare for the pain that comes with territory.

Learning everything I have over the last thirty-eight years I feel stripped. Stripped of anxiety that I will never be who I dreamed I would be at seven years old. I've come far. I've become who everyone doubted I would be. I can look myself in the mirror and honestly tell myself that I'm beautiful. But I can also look in the same mirror and know when I'm not having a good day and be ok with my flaws and all.

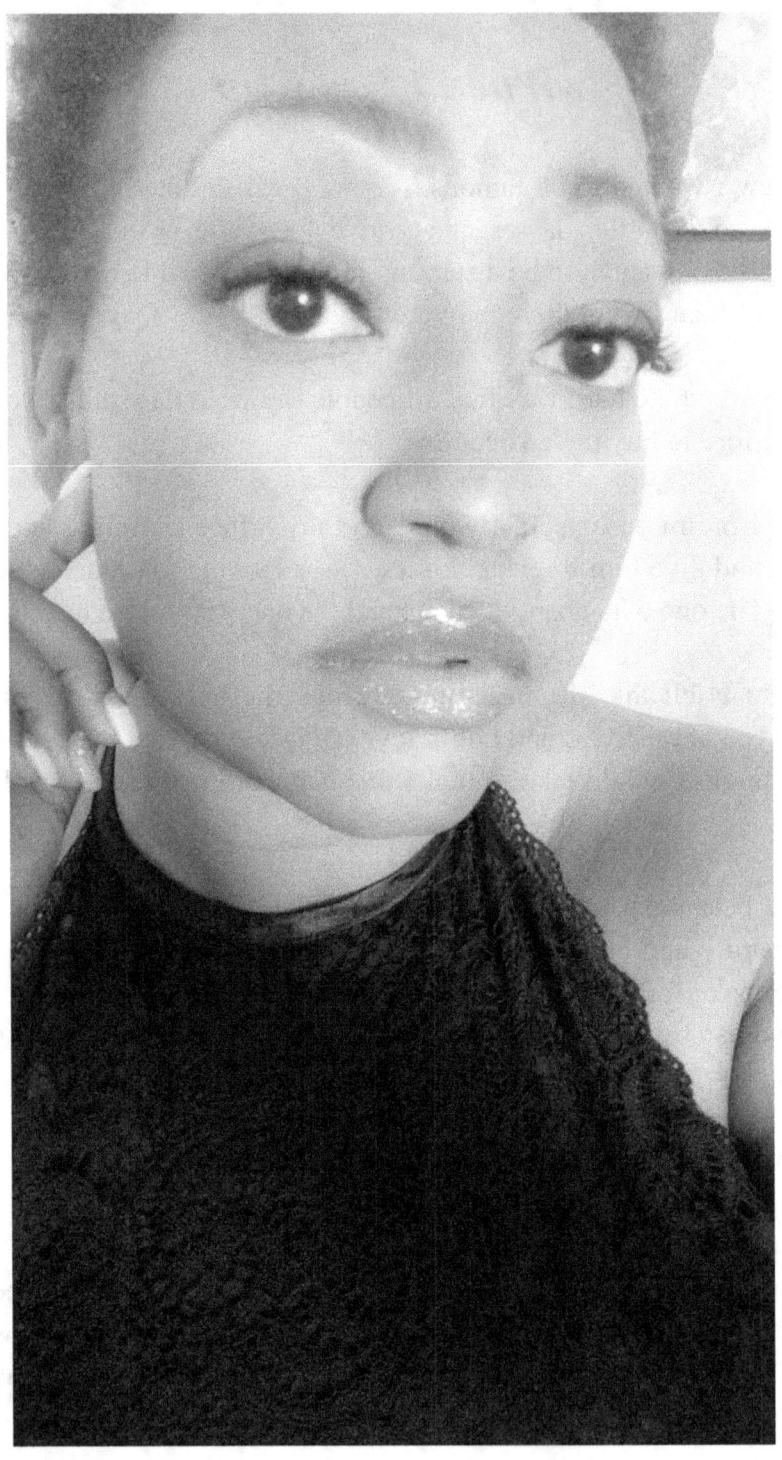

Labels

Fluffy

Fat

Thick

Plus Size

PHAT

Thicky Thick Girl

Curvy

They are all the same and come a dime a dozen.

The only label that matters is the word

BEAUTIFUL.

Feel it.

See it.

Be BeYOUtiful!

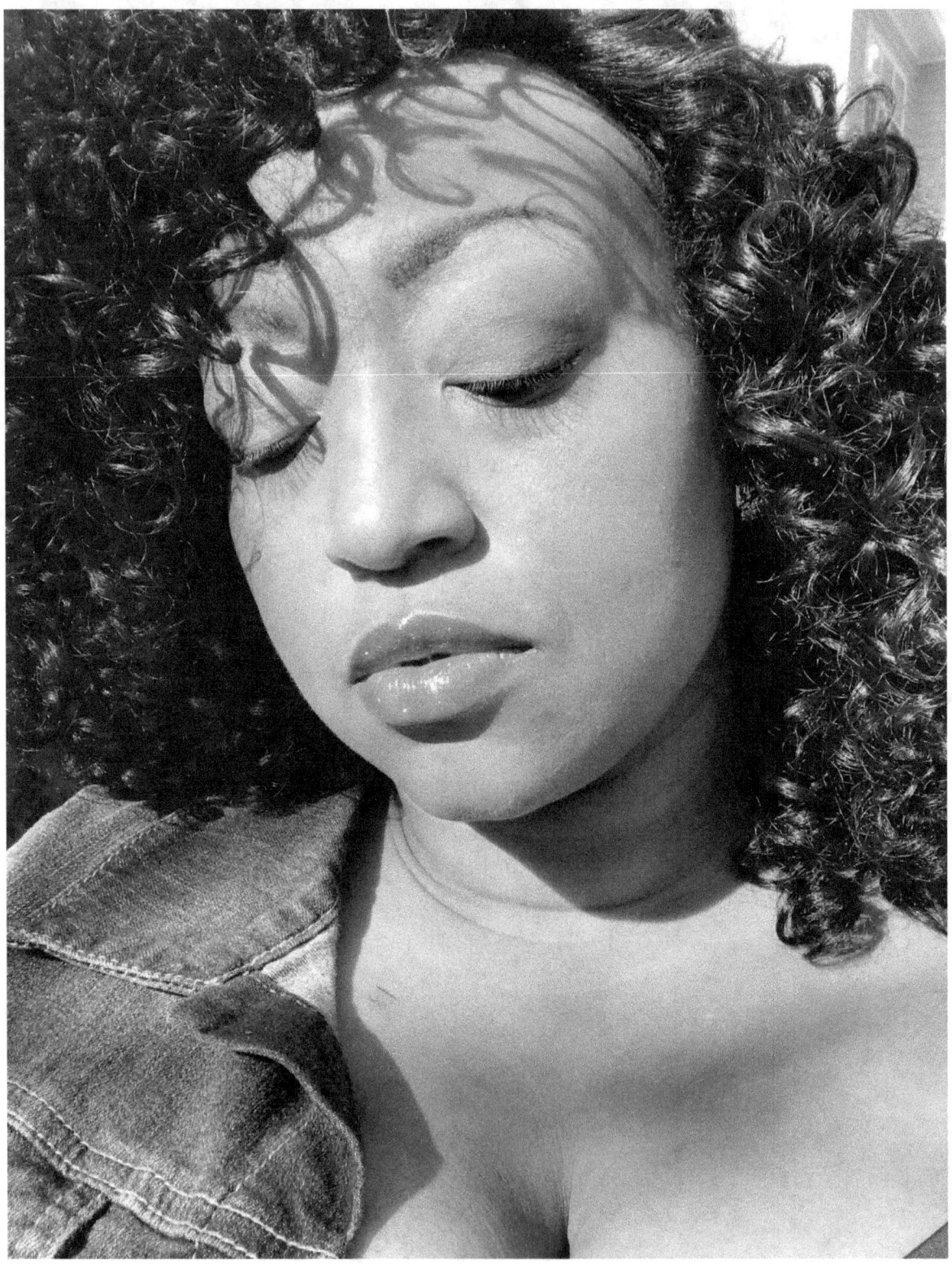

Naked Love

Take away all the eyelashes, makeup and wigs. Turn off all the cameras and social media.
Can you love me naked?

The most freeing thing is having somebody who loves me naked. He never asks for love but
takes it. He battles with me to break down my walls to see what's behind my flaws.
He loves me naked.

I'm a super bitch in the morning so he knows to offer me forehead kisses or to catch me at
night time. My attitude is a sassy one when I don't get my way. He sees my faults and
breaks them down every time. He is not afraid of loving me. When I'm being that bossy
bitch he loves so much, he knows how to put his foot down.
He loves me naked and eyes wide open.

Search for somebody who loves you when you look the most fucked up. Hold on to him
when he doesn't tell you how to feel and loves every beat of your heart. You will find his
love when he can't take his eyes off of you because he sees the real you.
His love for you is pure and naked.

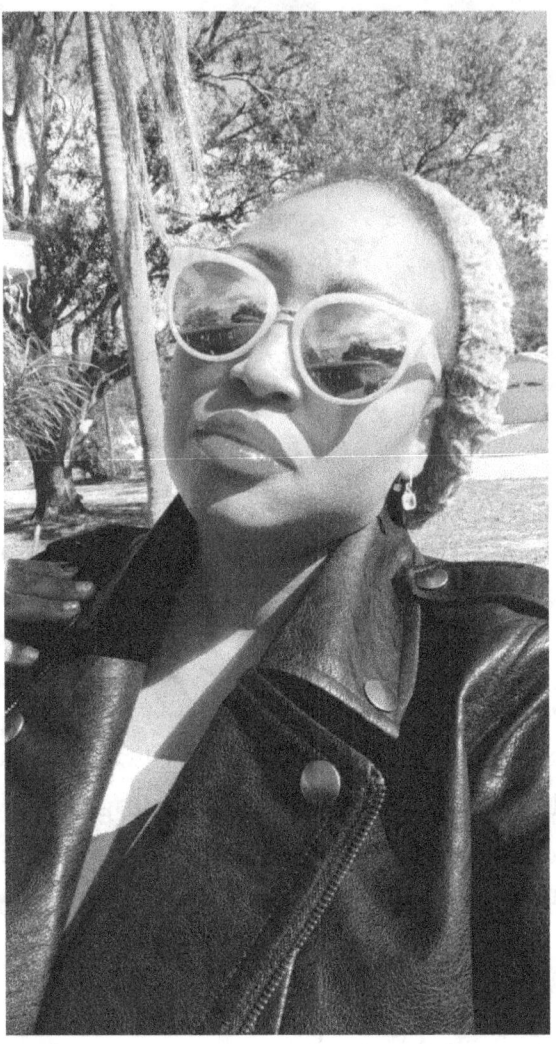

There is no cosmetic for beauty like happiness.

Maria Mitchell

Acknowledgements

This is me. This book. These pictures. These words. I'm not scared to be seen. When I starting thinking of this book it felt like dream. I didn't know were it would take me. I just keep telling myself if I inspired one person to love themselves more than I accomplished my goal of spreading love and light around the world. Through the tears and love from my family, friends and supporters "BeYOUtiful" was born.

Sidonia, Bonnie and Dawn, confidants and secret keepers, you have helped me so much over the last 14 years. You kept me out of jail. You've made me use my head when I wanted to use my heart to make life changing decisions. You are my "trifecta tribe". Your words are always kind and filled with truth and love.

My beta readers I apologize again for the all the tears I caused. I cried too.

To all the girls and women who feel they are alone in this big world full of people who don't look like you. Know that I look like you and we are beautiful. Head up buttercup. Walk with pride in know you are who God has made you to be. We warriors and we are glorious. Send a flood of goodness and love everywhere you go. Especially on social media. Live your best life and let nothing stand in your way.

My Cupcakes a.k.a. students. Thanks for cheering me on through this entire writing process. I listened to you. I heard your cries and wiped away some of you tears. This book is for you.

My book wife Nikki. Your gifs of love and joy fueled my fire to keep writing.

Selina and Alijah you keep me on my toes and working to make the world we live in a more loving place for us all. Your love surrounds me and keeps me climbing higher.

Coth my love and my best friend. I got you babe!

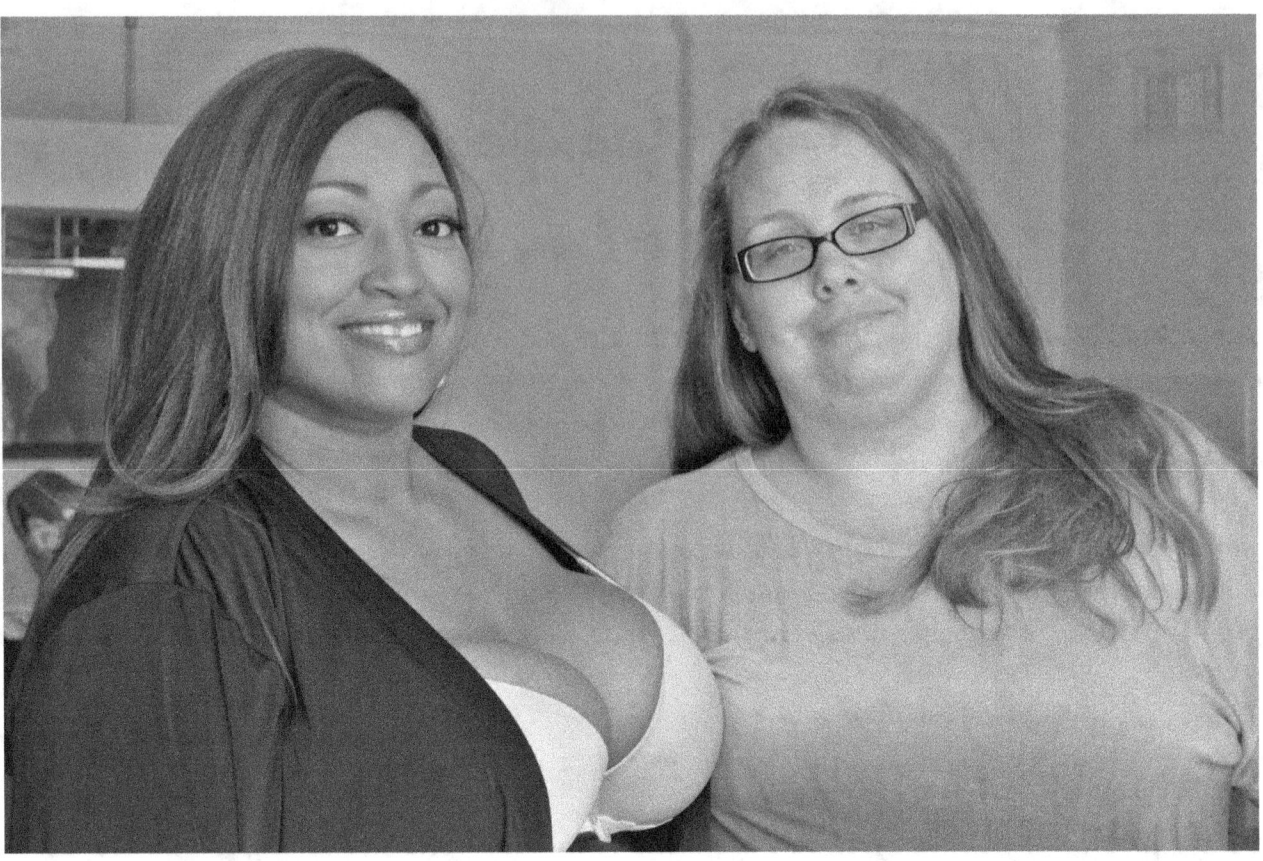

See this woman. This book is just as much her project of love as mine. Two years ago I decided to live a dream of becoming a model. At my age, yeah I know. But I always believe that everyone should live out their dreams no matter the obstacles. My stumbling block was that I couldn't find a photographer who believed in my dream. Then I was introduced to Melissa McAnuff. Our first shoot she made me feel like I belonged I front of the camera. Her pictures launched my career as beauty with plus model. Most of the pictures you find in this book were taken by her. When you have an incredible tribe no one can stand in your way. Melissa im blessed to have you in life. Thank you for believing in me and pushing boundaries with me.

Melissa Lynn Photography of Florida
Http://melissasattlerphotography.webs.com

About Martha

Thank you so much for reading my book. It was a project of self discovery and self love. I hope you love it and share it with the universe.

More by Martha Cothron

amazon.com/author/marthacothron

Social Links

Martha Boss-Model | Facebook

Instagram.com/MarthaBoss_model

Martha Cothron, Author | Facebook

Martha Boss (@MarthaBossModel) | Twitter

www.ingramcontent.com/pod-product-compliance
Lightning Source LLC
Chambersburg PA
CBHW081742220526
45468CB00008B/2202